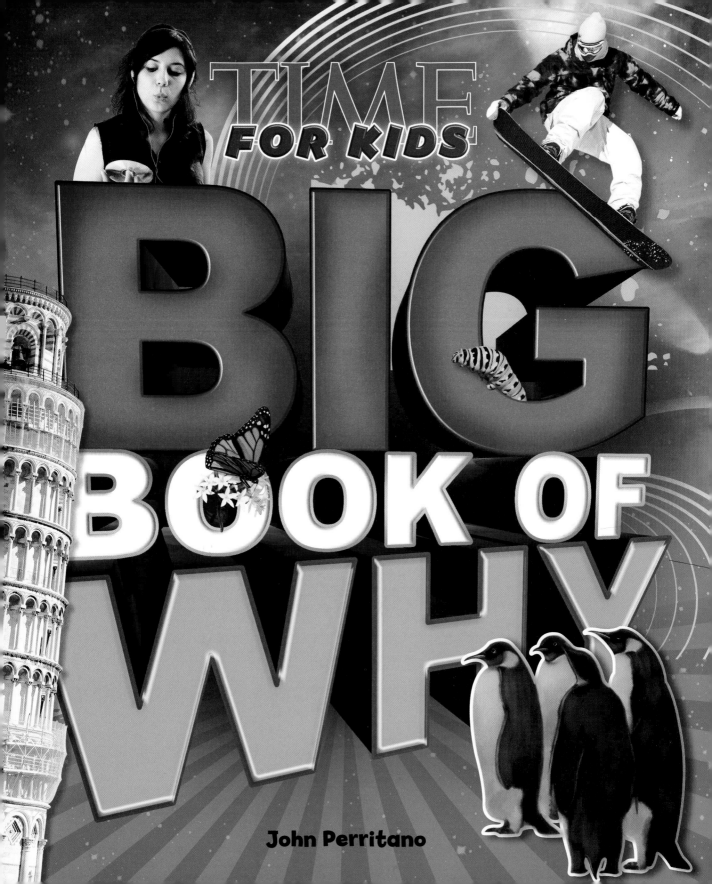

TIME FOR KIDS

BIG BOOK OF WHY

John Perritano

Time Home Entertainment
Publisher: Richard Fraiman
Vice President, Business Development & Strategy: Steven Sandonato
Executive Director, Marketing Services: Carol Pittard
Executive Director, Retail & Special Sales: Tom Mifsud
Executive Director, New Product Development: Peter Harper
Editorial Director: Stephen Koepp
Director, Bookazine Development & Marketing: Laura Adam
Publishing Director: Joy Butts
Finance Director: Glenn Buonocore
Assistant General Counsel : Helen Wan
Design & Prepress Manager: Anne-Michelle Gallero
Associate Brand Manager: Jonathan White
Associate Prepress Manager: Alex Voznesenskiy
Associate Production Manager: Kimberly Marshall

TIME For Kids
Managing Editor, TIME For Kids Magazine:
Nellie Gonzalez Cutler
Editor, TIME Learning Ventures: Jonathan Rosenbloom

Created by **Q2AMedia**
Publishing Director: Chester Fisher
Editor: Susan LaBella

Art Director: Harleen Mehta
Designer: Neha Kaul
Picture Researcher: Akansha Srivastava, Anubhav Singhal, Debabrata Sen, Nivisha Sinha, Tanmai Chaturvedi

Special Thanks: Christine Austin, Jeremy Biloon, Jim Childs, Susan Chodakiewicz, Rose Cirrincione, Jacqueline Fitzgerald, Christine Font, Jenna Goldberg, Lauren Hall, Carrie Hertan, Hillary Hirsch, Suzanne Janso, Raphael Joa, Mona Li, Amy Mangus, Robert Marasco, Amy Migliaccio, Nina Mistry, Dave Rozzelle, Ilene Schreider, Adriana Tierno, Lorin Driggs, Time Imaging

Copyright © 2010 Time Home Entertainment Inc.
All TIME For Kids material copyright © 2010 by Time Inc. TIME For Kids and the red border design are registered trademarks of Time Inc. For information on TIME For Kids magazine for the classroom or home, go to WWW.TIMEFORKIDS.COM or call 1-800-777-8600.

Published by TIME For Kids Books, an imprint of Time Home Entertainment Inc.
135 West 50th Street
New York, New York 10020

ISBN 10: 1-60320-842-9
ISBN 13: 978-1-60320-842-0
Library of Congress Control Number: 2010929003

TIME For Kids is a trademark of Time Inc.

We welcome your comments and suggestions about TIME For Kids Books. Please write to us at:
TIME For Kids Books
Attention: Book Editors
PO Box 11016
Des Moines, IA 50336-1016

If you would like to order any of our hardcover Collector's Edition books, please call us at 1-800-327-6388. (Monday through Friday, 7:00 a.m.— 8:00 p.m. or Saturday, 7:00 a.m.— 6:00 p.m. Central Time).

4 QGT 12

CONTENTS & QUESTIONS

ANIMALS 6

Why do some bugs glow in the dark?
Why do cats usually land on their feet?
Why do camels have humps?

EARTH 24

Why is the ocean salty?
Why is the ozone layer important?
Why is soil mostly brown?

SPACE 40

Why are planets round?
Why do some planets have rings and why
are they near each other?
Why can't we breathe in space?

HUMANS 56

Why does hair turn gray?
Why do I have a belly button?

Here's a look at some of the questions inside.

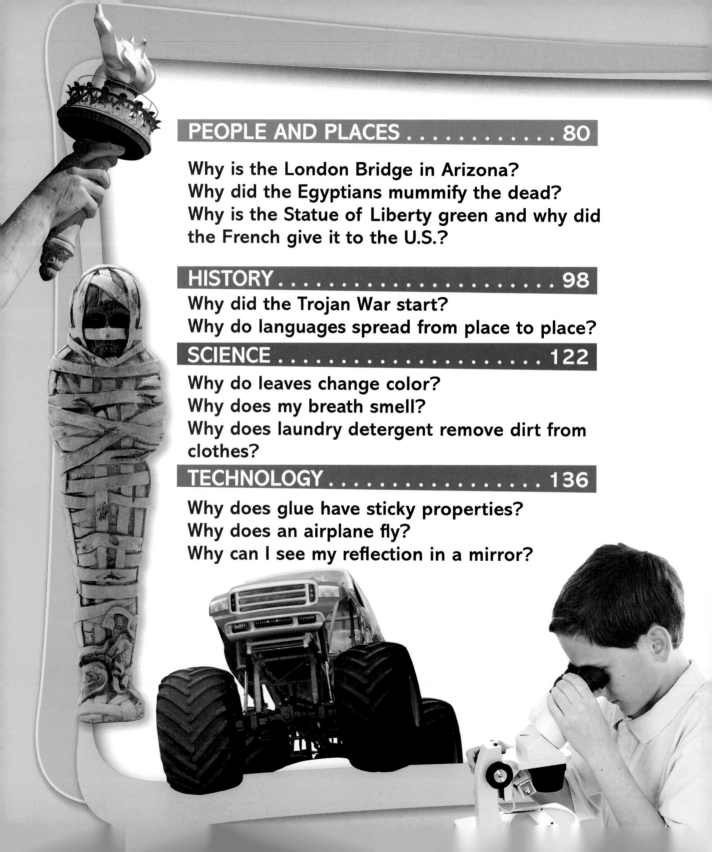

PEOPLE AND PLACES 80

Why is the London Bridge in Arizona?
Why did the Egyptians mummify the dead?
Why is the Statue of Liberty green and why did the French give it to the U.S.?

HISTORY 98

Why did the Trojan War start?
Why do languages spread from place to place?

SCIENCE 122

Why do leaves change color?
Why does my breath smell?
Why does laundry detergent remove dirt from clothes?

TECHNOLOGY 136

Why does glue have sticky properties?
Why does an airplane fly?
Why can I see my reflection in a mirror?

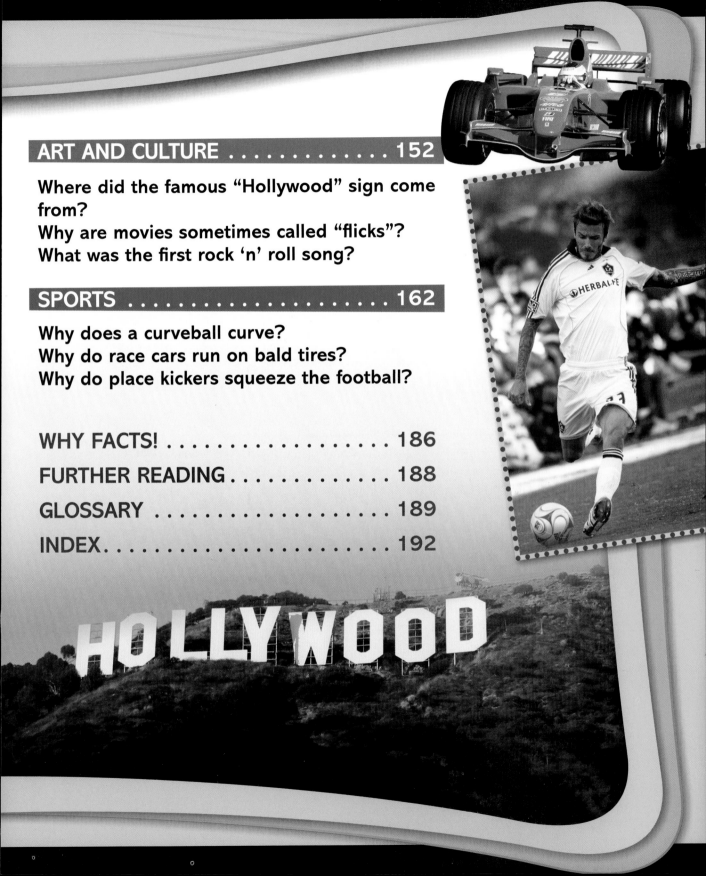

ART AND CULTURE 152

Where did the famous "Hollywood" sign come from?
Why are movies sometimes called "flicks"?
What was the first rock 'n' roll song?

SPORTS 162

Why does a curveball curve?
Why do race cars run on bald tires?
Why do place kickers squeeze the football?

WHY FACTS! 186

FURTHER READING 188

GLOSSARY 189

INDEX 192

HOLLYWOOD

Why are dogs' noses wet?

While the noses of many dogs are wet, plenty of dogs have dry ones. What keeps a dog's snout moist? No one knows for sure. One theory says that the wetness comes from **mucus** produced inside Fido's nose. Another **hypothesis** suggests that because dogs lick their noses all the time, saliva keeps their noses moist. Despite popular belief, a warm nose does not mean a dog is sick.

Why do dogs turn around before lying down?

Around, and around, and around again! Dogs will often circle the bed or carpet two or three times before curling up and going to sleep. Are they checking for bed bugs or snakes? Not necessarily. Many times dogs are just flattening out their beds to get comfortable. Actually, this behavior is a genetic trait left over from when the dog's ancestors used to dig their own shelters. After digging, the dogs would feel comfortable in their "dens" and plop down for some much needed shut-eye.

WHY DO WOLVES AND DOGS OFTEN LOOK ALIKE?

Scientists say that dogs evolved from wolves about 15,000 years ago. After comparing dog and wolf **DNA**, scientists say that every dog—from Chihuahuas to Great Danes—are descended from approximately five female Asian wolves. They are the mothers of all modern dogs.

Why do monkeys and apes prefer bananas **over other food?**

Monkeys and apes don't monkey around when they eat bananas. They really do enjoy the treat. Although monkeys and apes like eating other fruit, bananas seem to be tops on the menu. Bananas have a sweet smell and, well, taste great. Monkeys and apes like to use their thumbs to pull back the peel, too. It's like playing.

What makes apes **and monkeys different?**

Although apes and monkeys are both **primates**, a special kind of **mammal**, they are also different from one another..

MONKEYS	APES
Live in Africa, Asia, Central and South America;	Live mostly in Africa;
Tails allow them to live near the tops of trees;	Do not have tails; live mostly on the ground;
Smaller in size, usually weighing no more than 30 pounds.	Much bigger than monkeys; have broad backs;
	Can learn sign language and use tools, such as sticks and rocks.

An adult gorilla can weigh up to 452 pounds (205 kg).

WHY ARE APES SO MUCH LIKE HUMANS?

We might look a little different than a gorilla or any of the other Great Apes, but humans and apes have many things in common. We share about 99 percent of our genes with apes, and according to some scientists, apes—chiefly chimpanzees—form cultures just like humans. A culture is a learned way of living passed down from one generation to the next. Most researchers agree that humans and chimps diverged from a common ancestor about 5 to 7 million years ago.

Why do vampire bats drink blood?

There are many different types of bats, but there's only one type that drinks blood—the vampire bat. They are the only mammals that feed entirely on blood. A special **enzyme** in the saliva of a vampire bat keeps the blood of animals from clotting, making the blood easier to drink. Scientists say the first vampire bats that emerged were related to bats that gorged themselves on the parasites of prehistoric beasts. Vampire bats slowly evolved into drinking the blood of animals.

WHY DO BATS USE ECHOLOCATION?

Bats, which have poor eyesight, use echolocation to keep from slamming into objects and to detect their favorite meal—bugs. Bats emit a high frequency sound that humans cannot hear and then wait for the sound to echo off of any nearby objects. Based on how long the echo takes to reach it, bats can determine the distance, location, movement, and size of the object. Submarines use sonar in much the same way.

Why do **vampire bats rarely attack humans?**

Vampire bats would rather feast on sleeping animals than humans. Vampire bats live in the tropics of Central and South America. One hundred vampire bats can drink the blood of 25 cows in one year. Vampire bats do not remove enough blood to kill an animal, but the bites can cause an infection.

How many different kinds of fish are there?

There are more than 24,000 known species of fish living in the world's oceans, lakes, streams, ponds, and rivers. Fish were the first **vertebrates** to appear on Earth. Each species evolved over millions of years, adapting to its specific environment.

WHY CAN'T FISH BREATHE WHEN OUT OF WATER?

As with humans, fish need oxygen to live. Humans take in oxygen from the air. Fish can't breathe out of water because their bodies can't get oxygen from air. They can only get oxygen from water. The water passes through the mouth of the fish. The water then moves through a set of gills. The gills absorb oxygen from the water, just as our lungs absorb oxygen from the air.

WHY DO SOME FISH LIVE ONLY IN FRESHWATER AND OTHERS ONLY IN SALTWATER?

Evolution is the reason why some fish can live only in freshwater, while other fish live only in salty seawater. However, some fish live in both types of water. Some species began as saltwater fish, but later developed ways to live in freshwater.

This freshwater fish wouldn't live long in salt water!

How are crocodiles and alligators different?

Although they look like they are brother and sister, crocodiles and alligators are distant cousins.

ALLIGATORS

Live in the United States and China;

Have wide, U-shaped snouts;

Prefer to live in freshwater habitats.

CROCODILES

Live in Mexico, Central America, South America, Africa, Southeast Asia and Australia;

Have V-shaped snouts;

Prefer to live in saltwater habitats.

WHY ARE CROCODILES GOOD SWIMMERS?

The tail of a crocodile is huge and strong. In the water, crocodiles use their tails for power. Crocodiles swim by pressing their legs flat against their bodies, creating fish-like figures. Using one webbed foot as a rudder, they propel themselves forward by moving their strong tails back and forth. Crocodiles can swim up to 6.21 miles (10 km) per hour.

Female crocodiles can lay 25 to 80 eggs!

Alligators have been around for 150 million years.

Why do some bugs glow in the dark?

Who doesn't love glow-in-the-dark Halloween costumes, stickers, or glow sticks? Many bugs glow in the dark, too. They make their own light. These bugs are **bioluminescent** (by-oh-lew-muh-NESS-ent). Chemicals in their bodies combine to make them shine. Although bioluminescent animals light up, they don't give off heat like a light bulb does. Fireflies are the most common glow-in-the-dark insects. They light up to communicate with each other as they look for a mate.

WHY IS BIOLUMINESCENCE IMPORTANT?

Scientists study bioluminescence in animals for a number of reasons, including trying to find ways to cure cancer and other diseases in humans. For example, eye doctors use what scientists have learned about bioluminescence to detect, without using surgery, if an eye tumor is cancerous.

WHY DO SOME FISH GIVE OFF THEIR OWN LIGHT?

Deep in the ocean, some bioluminescent fish turn on the lights to attract their next meal. Other animals use light to blind predators that try to stalk and eat them. Some species create light to blend in with their surroundings. Scientists really don't know why some animals give off their own light. Some worms spit out glowing ooze, although no one can figure out why. It's a mystery why tiny plankton glow when disturbed by storms, waves, and passing boats.

Why do cats always land on their feet?

Cats are the acrobats of all household pets. If a cat falls from a short distance, it will almost always land on its feet. Because it lacks a collarbone, a cat can easily rotate and bend its body more than other animals. The backbones of cats are also more flexible than other animals. This allows them to turn and land on their feet.

Unlike dogs, cats have no problem landing on their paws.

WHY DO CATS COUGH UP HAIR?

Cough! Cough! Hack! Cats groom themselves by licking their fur. Naturally, they end up swallowing some hair in the process. When too much hair collects in a cat's stomach, the stomach lining becomes irritated and—*hack*!—the cat throws up a hairball.

Why do cats meow?

Cats can't talk, but they can certainly meow. And if they're *purrrrfectly* clear, humans know what they mean. One researcher says that cats have learned to meow in ways that call out to humans. Sometimes cats meow for attention. Such meows are very short and quiet (as in *ME-ow*). Sometimes a cat's meow is more urgent (as in me-*OWWW*). Cats also communicate with one another. They'll hiss when they are angry or feel threatened. They'll howl when they are hurt. Some big cats, like lions, don't meow at all. They roar!

Why can't penguins fly?

Penguins are odd—they have wings but can't fly like ordinary birds. Penguins belong to a group of birds call **sphenisciformes** (sfen-is-kuh-FORM-eez). Sphenisciformes would rather swim than fly. Penguins do not have hollow bones like flying birds. Instead, their bones are weighty, which makes it easier for them to dive into the water and swim. And penguins do love swimming. Adélie penguins can swim hundreds of miles at a steady 4.97 miles (8 km) per hour. Penguins use their wings to move through the water, just as any other bird uses its wings to move through the air.

HOW DOES A PENGUIN STAY WARM IN ANTARCTICA?

Penguins have a large amount of fat below their skin. The fat acts like insulation, keeping the torpedo-shaped critter warm even in the harsh climate of Antarctica. The birds have a special **circulatory system** in their feet. This keeps their bodies warm and their feet slightly cooler, reducing the amount of heat loss in the winter. Penguins also huddle with other penguins to keep toasty.

WHY DO MALE PENGUINS TAKE CARE OF THE PENGUIN EGGS?

During the cold months of Antarctica's winter, male emperor penguins huddle by the hundreds in the snow and ice. The females lay the eggs, and then the males keep the eggs warm on the tops of their feet for about 65 days. A layer of skin on the male's stomach hangs down over the egg to keep it warm. Where are the females during this period? After laying the eggs, the females go off to feed. When they return, they are fat and warm. After the eggs hatch, it's the male's turn to feast.

Why do fire ants sting?

Ouch! That burns! All ant bites and stings hurt, but the sting of a fire ant can be particularly painful. Fire ants are very aggressive and will swarm over anything and anyone that disturbs their nests, including wild animals, pets, and people. Fire ants have big jaws that can grab on to things and a bee-like stinger that pumps poison into their prey or an attacker. When their nests come under attack, or when the ants feel threatened, they will swarm. They give off special chemicals called **pheromones** (FEH-re-moans), which cause the ants to be overly aggressive. A red ant can sting many times. Its poison will cause a temporary burning feeling. When a group of red ants attack, their many stings can be deadly. The ants would have to sting an animal thousands of times for that to happen, however.

Red ants can carry up to 20 times their body weight!

Do ants have skeletons?

Although they don't have a bag of bones in their closets, ants do have skeletons—exoskeletons. Most animals—including you—have bones under the skin. But the skeleton of an ant is on the outside of its body. Exoskeletons are hard and protect the insect's soft insides.

WHY DO SOME ANTS HAVE WINGS?

Not all ants have wings, but some do. When you see an ant with wings, what you are seeing is an ant that is old enough to reproduce. Ants with wings are also known as *swarmers*. Their job is to fly to distant places and set up other ant colonies.

14

Why do spiders spin webs?

Spider-Man spins his web to swing from building to building and to catch villains. Real spiders spin webs for the same reasons—sort of. Spiders release a sticky type of silk from their **abdomens** when they spin a web. Spiders use webs to climb from place to place. Spiders also spin webs to trap their next meal and to make egg sacs to hold their eggs.

DO FEMALE BLACK WIDOW SPIDERS KILL THEIR MATES?

Most people believe the female black widow spider kills and then eats her mate after mating. This is not always the case. Males often escape the clutches of the female once they finish mating. However, on occasion, the female will eat the male.

What's the difference between **an arachnid** and an insect?

Many people call spiders insects, but that's not true. Spiders are arachnids and here is how they differ from insects:

Scorpions are also a type of arachnid.

ARACHNIDS	INSECTS
Have 8 legs and 8 eyes;	Have 6 legs and 2 compound eyes;
Do not have antennae or wings.	Have antennae and wings.

Why do some animals change color?

Many animals have developed ways to keep from getting eaten. One way is to change color. This type of **camouflage** helps animals hide from predators. Many animals produce chemicals inside their bodies that change their natural **pigments**. Many animals can change color anytime they want. A flounder for example, can change its color to match the mud, sand, and gravel on the ocean floor.

Flounders have a knack for blending into their surroundings.

Why do some animals protect other animals?

Some animals depend on one another to survive. This is called a **symbiotic** relationship. For example, the tiny clownfish hangs out with the poisonous sea anemone. The clownfish attracts food that the anemone likes to eat in return for the anemone's protection. The anemone's sting, however, does not harm the clownfish.

HOW DO STRIPES PROTECT A ZEBRA?

You might think that on the savannah of Africa, the black-and-white zebra stands out from the crowd, making it a tempting target for a passing lion. However, the zebra's stripes actually help the animal hide in plain sight. From a distance, a herd of zebras looks like a wavy mass of black and white lines, confusing a hungry lion. The lion can't pick out a single animal to attack, so the big cat retreats, leaving the zebras alone.

Flying squirrels don't really fly, they glide!

Why do squirrels have such **bushy tails?**

When a squirrel is in a tree it uses its big tail for balance. This helps the furry critter to move quickly from branch to branch without falling over. Squirrels also use their tails like parachutes in case they fall out of a tree. A squirrel's tail keeps the animal warm in the winter and allows the creature to communicate with other squirrels. A squirrel will threaten another squirrel by flinging its tail over its back and flicking it.

WHY DO SQUIRRELS EAT BIRDSEED?

Squirrels will often pounce on a birdfeeder because it is crammed with tasty nuts and seeds. Squirrels are primarily herbivores. They eat plant material such as nuts, fruits, mushrooms, pine cones, leaves, twigs, bark, and yes, birdseed.

DO SQUIRRELS REALLY REMEMBER WHERE THEY HIDE THEIR FOOD?

Let's put this myth to rest once and for all. Squirrels don't always remember where they hide their acorns and chestnuts. Scientists used to believe that squirrels, specifically gray squirrels, remembered where they dug their holes to store their nuts, and also smelled the food they buried. However, studies show that most of the squirrels never recover their buried nuts. In fact, other squirrels find the nuts and keep them. Most acorns and nuts remain buried and grow into young trees called saplings.

Why are some insects attracted to light?

Have you ever sat out on a front porch at night and turned on a light? What happens? Within moments, insects by the dozen start buzzing around the glowing bulb. There are a number of theories as to why bugs are attracted to light. Most scientists suspect that when an insect flies at night, it uses a light source, such as the moon, to keep on a straight path. If there is a closer source of light, such as a candle or light bulb, the insect gets confused, causing it to fly to the nearest light.

Why do some insects sting?

Some insects, such as bees, wasps, and ants, carry a loaded weapon with them at all times—a stinger full of poison. Bugs that sting are generally defending themselves or their nests. In most cases, a bee sting will only hurt for a while, unless a person is allergic to bee stings.

WHY DO MOSQUITOES BITE?

Mosquitoes have been around for 30 million years. During this time, they have become experts at finding people and animals on which to prey. Mosquitoes live off the blood of mammals. A mosquito is attracted to you by the warmth of your body and the chemicals that you exhale. Certain colored clothes can also make you a target.

Some mosquitoes can carry and spread diseases.

Why do bugs live on our bodies?

Not only do bugs live on your body, but they could make a home inside your body. Some bugs can crawl into your ears, dig into your skin, or feast on you while you sleep. Such creatures are parasites, organisms that live on– or in– another living being. Some bugs, such as lice and fleas, live outside your body. They are called ectoparasites. Other bugs, such as a tapeworm, may live inside your body. They are known as endoparasites. Most parasites such as lice, fleas, and bedbugs can be an annoying problem. Don't worry. It's very rare that a bug will set up camp on– or in– you.

WHY DO DOGS GET WORMS?

There are a lot of reasons why dogs get worms, and there are a lot of worms out there. Dogs can get roundworms from eating worm eggs off the ground. Dogs can get hookworms by licking their paws after they have touched the ground where hookworms live. Some dogs get tapeworms by eating fleas that swallowed tapeworm eggs.

Ticks are not insects. They're arachnids.

HOW DO SOME TICKS SPREAD DISEASE?

Ticks are tiny animals that feed on blood. Some are as small as a sesame seed. Some ticks, like the deer tick, can spread illnesses, such as Lyme disease, by transferring **bacteria** from animal to animal or animal to human.

Why are some animals domesticated?

Some animals, including cats, dogs, and horses are nice to have around the house or the barn. Such animals are **domesticated**. In other words, they have grown used to humans. Some scientists think that certain animals became domesticated through a series of genetic **mutations** that developed millions of years ago. Other scientists say that some animals found it easier to survive with humans around. The animals followed humans as they moved from place to place.

Why are there so many different kinds of dogs?

Why are some dogs tiny and some dogs big? Why do some dogs have lots of hair and others have very little or no hair? The American Kennel Club recognizes 157 dog breeds. Each breed has certain characteristics that developed over time through careful breeding. Dogs that evolved in colder climates have thick coats to keep them warm. Dogs such as the Chihuahua, that are native to warm climates, do not have much fur, allowing heat to escape more quickly. Some dogs are more muscular than others because they were bred to work. Some dogs are "mutts." Mutts are a mixture of many breeds. Mutts inherit characteristics from both parents.

HOW DO CATS PURR?

You've probably heard a cat purring—making a low rumbling sound as it breathes. A cat purrs when the muscles in its voice box vibrates. The muscles act as a valve for air flowing past the voice box. Cats purr when they inhale and exhale. Cats purr when they are happy or content. However, cats also purr when they are stressed out or recovering from an injury.

Why do giraffes have long necks?

Giraffes are the tallest mammals on the planet. Some stand up to 19 feet (5.79 m) high. Some scientists think giraffes have long necks to reach leaves high on trees, especially during periods of drought. Others say giraffes have long necks to help them fight. Male giraffes use their necks as weapons, clubbing their opponents with their heavy skulls.

WHY DO LEOPARDS HAVE SPOTS?

Don't get any spot remover near a leopard. Scientists say leopards evolved with dark spots to help them hide from their prey.

Why do camels have humps?

Someone might have told you long ago that the humps on camels contain water. *NOT TRUE!* The humps of camels are filled with fatty tissue. Animals, including humans, store energy in fat. When there's no food or water around, animals live off the stored fat. In the harsh dry desert, camels' fatty humps let them live for a long time without water.

21

Why do birds fly south for the winter?

Some birds—not all—pack their feathers for the winter and fly south where it is much warmer. These birds are not only searching for a warmer climate, but are also looking for food and water. The journey is known as **migration**. Before they start their trips, birds stuff themselves with food so they can store up fat that they will use as energy for their long journey.

WHY DO BIRDS HAVE FEATHERS?

All birds have feathers. In fact, birds are the only animals with feathers. Feathers keep birds warm. Feathers on wings help birds fly. Feathers on a bird's tail help it steer as it soars. Feathers also give a bird its colors. Some birds use feathers as camouflage. Some male birds, such as the peacock, use their feathers to attract a female.

Why do birds sing?

Whether it's the squawk of a crow or the squeak of a cardinal, birds like to sing. Birds hit the high notes not because they are fans of rock 'n' roll, but because they are communicating with each other. Each birdcall has a different meaning. Sometimes males sing to attract a female. Other times, a male is warning other birds to keep away from his nest. Most birds only pay attention to birds that sound and look like them.

How do **caterpillars** turn into **butterflies?**

When is a caterpillar not a caterpillar? When it is a butterfly. Caterpillars turn into butterflies through a process called **metamorphosis** (met-ah-MOR-fa-sis). There are four stages of a butterfly's metamorphosis.

1. The first stage is when the adult female butterfly lays her eggs.
2. The eggs then form a larva, which is the caterpillar. During this stage of metamorphosis, caterpillars have only one job—eat as much as possible. When caterpillars are fully grown, they stop eating.
3. Then they spin a cocoon. This is called the pupa stage. The pupa of a butterfly is called a chrysalis. The pupa hangs on a branch or a leaf.
4. Inside the cocoon, the caterpillar completely changes into the adult stage—a butterfly that breaks out of the cocoon and flies away.

Is it a **moth** or a **butterfly?**

Although similar, butterflies and moths have many differences.

BUTTERFLIES	MOTHS
Out during the day;	Out during the night;
Hold their wings above their body when they rest;	Hold their wings down flat when they rest;
Are very colorful.	Most are not very colorful.

WHY DO CICADAS BUZZ?

When summer rolls around, listen carefully. You might hear the buzz of the cicada. It sounds like an electric razor. Cicadas are insects that resemble huge flies. They buzz to attract a mate. The sound is produced by a pair of drum-like organs on the base of their abdomen. These organs vibrate at high speed, creating a buzzing sound that you hear generally between mid-July and September.

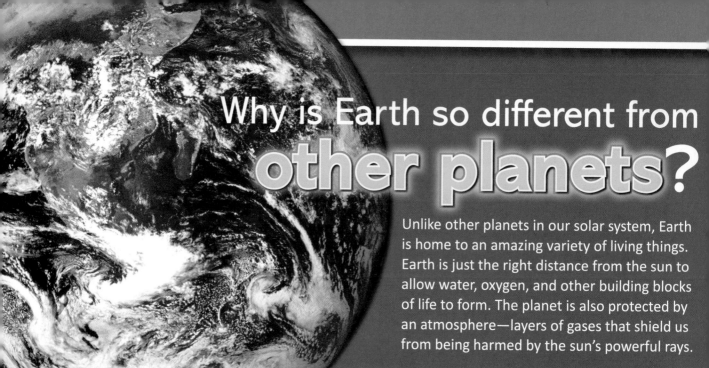

Why is Earth so different from other planets?

Unlike other planets in our solar system, Earth is home to an amazing variety of living things. Earth is just the right distance from the sun to allow water, oxygen, and other building blocks of life to form. The planet is also protected by an atmosphere—layers of gases that shield us from being harmed by the sun's powerful rays.

How did life form on Earth?

Scientists have many theories on how life formed on Earth. Some believe that life evolved near hydrothermal vents, deep holes in the ocean floor that spew heated water. Others say meteors rained down on the planet about a half billion years ago, seeding the Earth with molecules that triggered life.

WHY DO SOME CREATURES LIVE IN UNUSUAL PLACES?

There are some wacky places on Earth where creatures live. Organisms called extremophiles have adapted to life in places we might think are uninhabitable. These extremophiles live deep in the ocean where it is very dark and cold, or in the acidic waters of Yellowstone National Park.

Scientists study extremophiles to see what life might be like on Mars.

How do tornadoes form?

A tornado is a column of rapidly rotating air that generally begins life as a thunderstorm. The atmosphere becomes unstable when warm, moist air bangs into a wall of cool, dry air. Near the ground sits a layer of warm, humid air. In the upper atmosphere is a layer of cold air. The warm air rises. The cold air falls. A tornado is born when the wind's speed and direction causes the rising air to rotate vertically in the middle of the storm.

WHY DOES TORNADO ALLEY GET MORE TORNADOES THAN OTHER PLACES?

Tornado Alley is a part of the United States stretching from Texas to North Dakota. Although tornadoes occur throughout the U.S., they take place more often and with more force in Tornado Alley. Why is that? Tornado Alley is flat. It is also where warm, moist air from the Gulf of Mexico and cold, dry air from Canada collide. When that happens, tornadoes are born.

WHY ARE TORNADOES DANGEROUS?

Tornadoes are storms of swirling wind that are among the most violent in nature. Tornadoes can generate wind speeds of 250 mph (402.34 km) or more. As they move, tornadoes can sometimes cut a path of destruction a mile wide and more than 50 miles (80 km) long. Once a tornado picked up a motel sign in Oklahoma and dropped it 30 miles (48 km) away in Arkansas.

Why can astronauts see the Grand Canyon from space?

The Grand Canyon is more than a big hole in the ground. It is a wonder of nature. The canyon is 277 miles (445.8 km) long, up to 18 miles (29 km) wide, and one mile (1.6 km) deep. Although other forces were at work, the rushing water of the Colorado River carved out the canyon over millions of years. The Grand Canyon is so huge that astronauts can see it from space without a telescope.

WHY DOES THE GRAND CANYON GET SO COLD AT NIGHT?

The Grand Canyon is in the desert. During a summer day, the bottom of the canyon can get extremely hot, with temperatures reaching more than 100°F (38°C). Deserts have very dry air that holds little moisture and heat. As soon as the sun sets, the air cools, especially at the rim of the canyon, causing a big temperature change.

Why is the Grand Canyon colorful?

The Grand Canyon looks as if someone piled up layers of colorful rock. As the rocks eroded over thousands and thousands of years, the minerals in the rocks created different colors including reds, browns, and oranges.

Lava can get as hot as 2,000°F (1,100°C).

WHY DO PEOPLE GET SICK WHEN A VOLCANO ERUPTS?

A volcano's ash and dust can cause breathing problems. Volcanoes also spew poison gas into the air. The Kilauea Volcano in Hawaii vents about 1,800 tons (1,632.93 MT) of sulfur dioxide a day. The ash and dust can harm drinking water, and create volcanic smog called "vog" that makes it hard to see.

How does a volcano work?

Think of a volcano as a soda can. Shake the can, and gas and pressure build up inside. Open the top and *bam!*—an explosion occurs. Volcanoes work much the same way. The heat deep inside Earth is so intense that it melts rock and creates explosive gases. Scientists call that molten rock magma. Magma slowly rises to the surface, collecting in underground chambers. Eventually, the pressure of the magma becomes so great that it pushes through Earth's crust. Soon a volcano is blowing its top.

WHY SHOULDN'T I TOUCH LAVA?

Lava is just another name for magma that reaches the surface of the Earth. If you find yourself close enough to a volcano where you can touch the lava, run as fast as you can! Lava is hot, hot, hot! How hot? It can reach temperatures of 2,000°F (1,100°C). A volcano can shoot lava into the air up to 2,000 feet (609.6 m).

Why do **earthquakes destroy** some **buildings** and not others?

During an earthquake, the ground shakes, twists, and heaves, causing buildings to move. Houses can shift on their foundations, crack, and tumble to the ground. Some buildings, however, are built to withstand violent earthquakes. Some are also braced with special materials to keep them standing.

HOW DO SCIENTISTS MEASURE THE STRENGTH OF AN EARTHQUAKE?

In 1933, Dr. Charles Richter came up with a way to compare the strength of earthquakes—the Richter scale. Scientists give each earthquake a numeric rating on a scale of 0 to 6.0. Each number on the scale represents how much the ground shakes. Each number is 10 times greater than the number before it. For example, a 6.0 **magnitude** quake has 10 times more motion than a 5.0 magnitude quake.

How do tectonic plates move?

Earth's outermost layer is separated into a dozen or so tectonic plates, enormous slabs of Earth's crust that slowly move across the surface of the planet. The plates move by riding on top of the Earth's hot **mantle**. The tectonic plate movement varies from 4 to 6 inches (0.10 to 0.15 m) per year.

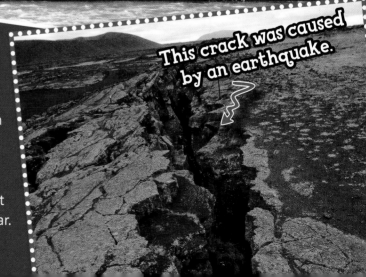

This crack was caused by an earthquake.

WHY CAN I FLOAT IN THE OCEAN?

Salt in the ocean makes the water denser, or thicker. The denser the water, the easier it is to float on it.

Why is the ocean salty?

A Norwegian folktale says ocean water is salty because a mill at the bottom of the ocean is grinding out salt. The truth is the ocean gets its salt from rocks on land. When rain falls, it erodes the rocks. The water dissolves minerals from the rocks, including chloride and sodium (the main ingredients in salt). Those minerals flow down streams and rivers into the ocean.

Why shouldn't I drink sea water?

First, it tastes yucky. Second, it causes **dehydration**. If you drink salt water, your body would have to get rid of more water than you drank in order to push out the extra salt. As a result, you would be thirstier than you were before.

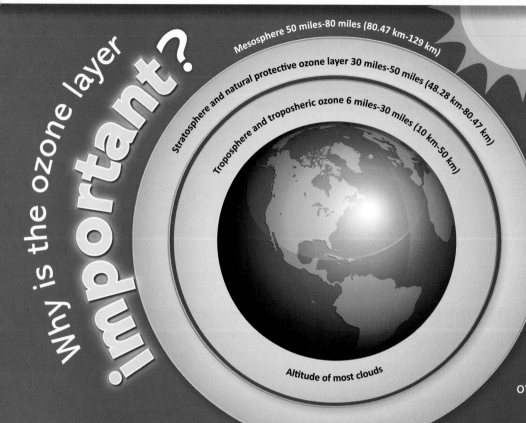

Mesosphere 50 miles-80 miles (80.47 km-129 km)

Stratosphere and natural protective ozone layer 30 miles-50 miles (48.28 km-80.47 km)

Troposphere and troposheric ozone 6 miles-30 miles (10 km-50 km)

Altitude of most clouds

Earth's atmosphere protects the planet from many things, including the sun's harmful rays. The sun bathes Earth in **ultraviolet radiation** that can damage our eyes and skin. The atmosphere's **ozone layer** absorbs much of this radiation.

Why does the atmosphere "breathe"?

Just like us, the atmosphere needs to breathe every once in a while. Scientists discovered in 2008 that Earth's atmosphere expands and contracts every nine days or so—in other words, it breathes. They say the solar wind, highly charged atomic particles produced by the sun, causes the atmosphere to expand and contract.

WHY IS IT MORE DIFFICULT TO BREATHE AT HIGHER ALTITUDES?

At high altitudes, a mile (1.61 km) or more above sea level, the air is thinner. That doesn't mean the air is actually thin. It means there's less oxygen available at that height. Air pressure decreases the higher you go. For your lungs to fill with air, the air pressure in your lungs has to be less than the pressure of the air outside. When it's not, breathing becomes strained.

Why don't you feel upside down in Antarctica?

Relative to the rest of the world, people and penguins in Antarctica are upside down. In fact, people living in New York and London walk around in a tilted position, while people on the equator stand sideways. Still, we all feel as though we are standing straight up. Why is that? Earth's **gravity** pulls us toward Earth's center. If the world was flat, we would all experience the same "downward" direction. Since Earth is a sphere, Earth's center is straight down from wherever you are standing. So, people are tilted or upside down with respect to each other, even though they think they are upright.

Why don't we fall off the planet?

There are many forces that want to fling us into outer space. The gravitational force of the moon tries to pull us off the planet as does Earth spinning on its axis. Yet, gravity is always pulling us toward the center of the Earth. Earth's gravity is so strong that it keeps our feet on the ground.

Earth's gravity causes quakes on asteroids that are passing 30 million miles (48.3 million km) away.

WHY DOESN'T EARTH FLY OFF INTO SPACE?

Once again, gravity saves the day. This time, though, it is the sun's gravitational tug, and the gravitational pull from the other planets, that keeps Earth anchored in its orbit.

Why is air in spray cans cold?

People use canned air to clean dust from computer keyboards, cameras, and other items. Canned air is not the same as the air you breathe. Canned air is usually a combination of nitrogen and other gases. When a gas is placed under a high amount of pressure and then released, there is a tremendous drop in temperature. The surrounding air and the can itself get cold as the gas expands outward. Don't spray canned air on your skin. You might get frostbite. Always use canned air with a parent's okay.

Why can't we see air?

Air is all around us, but we can't see it. That's because Earth's atmosphere is made up of several gases including oxygen, water vapor, and carbon dioxide. The molecules of these gases don't absorb light that our eyes can see, so air is invisible to us.

WHY DOES HOT AIR CAUSE A BALLOON TO RISE?

When air is heated, its molecules move faster. The faster the molecules move, the more space they take up. Because hot air is less dense than cold air, the hot air "floats" on top of the cold air, causing the balloon to rise. When the air inside the balloon cools, the balloon goes down.

Why does the ocean have waves?

Have you ever tried to catch a wave? It's pretty hard. Winds create waves on oceans and lakes. When the wind blows, it transfers some of its energy to the water. **Friction** between the air molecules and water molecules creates a wave.

HOW DO TIDES FORM?

Tides form when the moon's gravitational pull tugs on Earth's oceans. When that happens, the sea rises toward the moon. High tides occur on the side of the Earth facing the moon. Low tides occur on the side of Earth facing away from the moon.

Why are tsunamis so dangerous?

Tsunamis are monster ocean waves caused by underwater earthquakes, volcanic eruptions, or landslides. The energy created by these geological disturbances spreads outward from the **epicenter**. Large volumes of water, known as swells, also move from the center. The swells become high waves as they bunch up in shallow water near the shore. By that time the monster wave might have grown as high as 164 feet (50 m) or more.

33

Why isn't the sky black, purple, or green?

It might be cool to have a green sky for a day or two, but don't count on that happening. During a clear day, the sky is blue. Why is that? Light from the sun, which is made up of different rainbow colors, has to pass through atoms of nitrogen and oxygen in the atmosphere. Because those atoms are so tiny, they cause light to break up. The atoms break up the color blue much more easily than they do other colors.

WHY DO CLOUDS FLOAT?

Clouds float because the cloud is warmer than the air around it.

How do clouds get their shapes?

Some clouds look like animals. Others look like people. Some even look like old cars. Clouds form when heated air rises. As it slowly cools, water vapor condenses to form a cloud. Clouds get their shapes when swirling air pushes them in different directions. Clouds really don't look like animals or people. It's just that we have fun trying to see shapes in clouds.

Why do people sink in quicksand?

Quicksand is just an ordinary mixture of sand and clay that becomes water-logged, reducing friction between the sand particles. Such a mushy mixture cannot support weight. Quicksand itself won't suck you down, but you can get stuck in it. Moving will cause you to sink deeper. But don't despair—quicksand is generally only a few feet deep. How do you get out of quicksand? The best thing to do is to move slowly. If you struggle, you'll sink. If you relax and try to lie on your back, you can get yourself out of this mess.

Why is soil mostly brown?

Sometimes soil is red, yellow, or even black. Most soil, however, is brown. Soil is created by the way plants and animals **decompose**. Over time, dead trees, flowers, and even bits of food break down, or rot. Organic material that decomposes leaves behind minerals. They give soil its color. Different colors show different minerals. Red soil, for example, is high in iron.

WHY DO SINKHOLES FORM?

When rock under the soil wears away, it can leave huge spaces underground. Suddenly, the soil collapses—a sinkhole is born. Sinkholes come in various sizes. They are mainly caused by water circulating underground that dissolves the surrounding rock. Some sinkholes are big enough to swallow up entire buildings.

Why do flags **wave** and tree branches **sway?**

Look outside. Can you see tree branches moving or a flag waving? If so, the wind is blowing. Wind is moving air formed by pressure differences in the atmosphere. **Air pressure** is caused by differences in temperature. Warm temperatures expand air molecules, causing air to weigh less and creating low air pressure. Cold temperatures press air molecules together, causing high air pressure. Wind begins to blow when air molecules flow from high pressure areas to low pressure areas.

HOW CAN IT BE 8 A.M. IN NEW YORK WHEN IT'S 2 P.M. IN FRANCE?

Welcome to the wonderful world of time zones. Humans created time zones—a uniform standard of time—because of Earth's rotation. Only one section of the globe faces the sun at any given time. As one side of Earth has daylight, the other side of the planet is having nighttime. There are 24 times zones because it takes Earth 24 hours to make one complete turn on its axis.

Why is it **winter** in Detroit, Michigan, while it's **summer** in Sydney, Australia?

Because Detroit is in the Northern Hemisphere, and Sydney is in the Southern Hemisphere, the seasons are reversed. Why is that? Earth tilts on its axis as it moves around the sun. When it's wintertime in Detroit, or anywhere else in the Northern Hemisphere, Earth is tilted away from the sun. So, the sun's rays indirectly strike the Northern Hemisphere, causing winter conditions. At the same time, Australia and the rest of the Southern Hemisphere are tilted more toward the sun. The sun's rays strike the Southern Hemisphere more directly, resulting in summer conditions.

The colors in this satellite photo show different hurricane wind speeds near Florida.

Why are hurricane winds so powerful?

The wind from a hurricane can rip buildings from their foundations and knock trees down. Hurricanes have winds that blow at least 74 miles (119.09 km) per hour. Hurricanes are fueled by warm ocean water. When a storm passes over warm water, the strong rotational movement of Earth causes the moist air over the ocean to spiral upward. As the air rises, it cools and falls as rain. The heat given off when the air condenses creates huge amounts of energy, causing a hurricane to form.

WHY CAN'T SCIENTISTS STOP HURRICANES?

Hurricanes are so massive that they are impossible to stop or weaken. During the 1960s, the National Oceanic and Atmospheric Administration (NOAA) tried various ways to weaken hurricanes, but they could not stop the huge storms.

WHY WAS HURRICANE KATRINA SO DEADLY?

When Hurricane Katrina passed over the Gulf Coast in 2005, the storm killed many people. Most of the deaths were in New Orleans where a **storm surge**—a massive wall of water—overwhelmed the city's **levees** that held back water from Lake Pontchartrain and the Mississippi River. New Orleans, which lies below sea level, flooded. At least 1,836 people died during the storm, and entire neighborhoods along the Gulf Coast were destroyed.

Why is Mount Everest so tall?

Some 250 million years ago, India, Africa, Australia, and South America were all one continent that scientists call Pangea. About 60 million years ago, the tectonic plate that India sits on moved northward, charging across the equator at roughly 5.91 inches (15 cm) a year. Eventually, India slammed into Asia. The collision erased an ocean named the Tethys Sea. The colliding plates and the sinking ocean floor pushed up the Himalaya Mountains, including what became Mount Everest, the tallest mountain in the world.

Why are Earth's ice caps melting?

The heat is on in Antarctica and the Arctic. Global warming, an overall rise in Earth's temperature, is melting the polar ice caps. The rise in temperatures is causing huge chunks of Antarctic ice to fall into the ocean. In the Arctic, polar bears are finding their icy territories melting, causing the beautiful bears to be endangered.

WHY ARE THE HIGHEST MOUNTAINS NEAR THE EQUATOR?

Mountains form when tectonic plates slam into one another. That force, coupled with **erosion**, determines the height of mountain ranges. Scientists say **glaciers** play a major role, too. The closer a mountain is to Earth's poles, the easier it is for glaciers to cut mountains down to size. Peaks are higher near the equator because glaciers don't impact the mountains there as much.

Why does Earth have different types of rocks?

Earth rocks! While there are many different types of rocks on the planet, they fall into only three categories: igneous, metamorphic, and sedimentary.

- Igneous rocks, such as pumice, form when molten rock reaches Earth's surface and cools.
- Metamorphic rocks, such as marble, are created when heat and pressure bind different rocks together.
- Sedimentary rocks, such as limestone, form when sediment builds up and is compacted.

Metamorphic Rock

Sedimentary Rock

Igneous Rock

WHY ARE SOME ROCKS HARDER THAN OTHERS?

Rocks are made from minerals. The harder the minerals, the harder the rock will be. Diamonds are the hardest rocks on the planet, talc the softest.

Why are diamonds so rare?

Diamonds form when carbon deep below Earth's surface is squeezed under tremendous pressure. Diamonds are uncommon because pressure seldom pushes the gems to the surface. In fact, only 350 tons (317,515 kg) of diamonds have ever been mined.

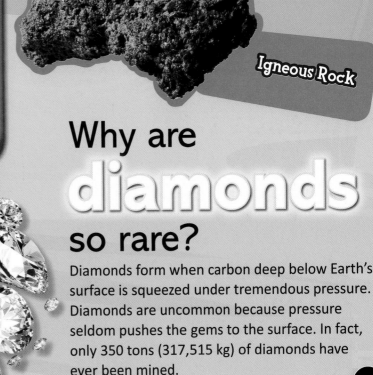

Why are planets round?

People once thought Earth was flat. Then someone figured out that Earth and the other planets were round. Planets are round due to gravity's pull. As planets form, **gravity** pulls **matter** inward toward the center of the planet. When that happens, every part of the planet is pulled evenly toward the center, giving the planet its spherical shape. Not all planets are truly round, however. Because Earth is spinning, gravity forces the planet to have a slight bulge in its mid-section.

Why are stars invisible during the day?

f you live in Hollywood, you see stars all the time—even during the day. However, most people see only one star during daylight hours—our sun. The sun's brightness during the day blocks out the light from other stars.

WHY DO STARS TWINKLE?

Stars really don't twinkle, it just looks that way. Stars appear to twinkle because we view them through thick layers of hot and cool air in Earth's atmosphere. Since the air is moving, the light of the star bends as it travels through the atmosphere. Each time you look at the star, the path of its light has changed slightly, giving the illusion that it twinkles.

WHY DO SCIENTISTS STUDY COMETS?

Many scientists say comet dust contains the building blocks of planets, including carbon, hydrogen, and oxygen. These are some of the elements that went into forming Earth 4 billion years ago. NASA—the U.S. space agency—even sent a space probe to bring back a bit of comet dust for study. When the probe, *Stardust* (right), returned to Earth, scientists discovered the ancient building blocks of the solar system that they were looking for.

WHY DO COMETS HAVE NAMES?

Comets are named for those who first discovered them. In the late 1980s, about a dozen comets were discovered each year. Now, about 30 comets a year are found because there are more people looking for them. Sometimes, comets have combined names like Hale-Bopp. That's because more than one person discovered the comet.

Why do comets' tails look like they're on fire?

Comets are dirty snowballs—huge lumps of frozen water, carbon dioxide, methane, and ammonia. When a comet gets close to the sun, the heat of the sun causes the ice to melt, forming a long, dusty tail. When a comet moves away from the sun, its tail disappears.

Why is the sun so bright?

The sun is a big ball of super-heated gas that generates as much energy every second as all the power plants on Earth could produce in about 2 million years! The sun gets its enormous energy through fusion, a nuclear reaction that joins together the **nuclei** of atoms. Fusion takes place deep inside the sun at temperatures of 27 million°F (15 million°C). Fusion converts hydrogen to helium and releases energy, which makes the sun very bright and able to give off so much light and heat.

WHY DON'T PLANETS FLY OFF INTO SPACE?

The sun is gigantic—roughly 333,000 times the size of Earth! Something that big has a lot of mass and therefore a lot of gravity. The sun's gravitational pull, coupled with the sideways motion of the planets, is why the planets orbit the sun and why everything in the solar system doesn't crash into the sun or fly off into outer space.

Why does the sun have spots?

Sunspots are relatively cool areas on the sun's surface. The spots are about 5,840°F (3,227°C). They are created when strong **magnetic fields** rise from the sun's interior to the surface. These magnetic fields interrupt the normal process that brings energy to the sun's surface and makes it bright and hot. Sunspots are roughly 30,000 miles (48,000 km) wide.

Why can I sometimes see the moon during the day?

You can see the moon during the day—and at night— because the sun's light is reflecting brilliantly off the moon's surface. In addition, the moon is close to Earth, only 238,000 miles (383,000 km) away, which makes it easier to see on some days.

Scientists found water on the moon in 2009.

WHY IS IT WE NEVER SEE THE OTHER SIDE OF THE MOON?

Every time you look at the moon do you notice something familiar? It always looks the same. Why is that? The moon and Earth are locked in **synchronous rotation**. In other words, it takes the same amount of time for the moon to orbit Earth as it takes for the moon to rotate on its axis. That means the same side of the moon that faces the Earth would be in view day and night.

Why does the moon appear to change its shape?

As the moon orbits Earth each month, our view of the moon changes. Half of the moon is always sunlit, but the position of the moon and Earth compared to the sun determines how much of the sunlit areas we can see each night.

WHY IS THE MOON POCKMARKED WITH CRATERS?

Falling asteroids and meteorites created thousands of craters on the moon's surface. Unlike Earth, the moon does not have a protective atmosphere that destroys most meteors before they strike the ground.

Why do we call Mars the "Red Planet"?

We should really call Mars the "Rusty Planet." Its soil is rich in iron oxides, known to Earthlings as rust. Iron oxides are chemical **compounds** made up of iron and oxygen that give off a reddish color. Some ancient people used to think that blood caused the reddish glow of Mars.

WHY WOULDN'T WE BE ABLE TO BREATHE ON MARS?

The atmosphere on Mars is made up mostly of carbon dioxide, a gas which trees on Earth love but is poisonous to humans.

Why are there canals on Mars?

Although many people used to think that Mars had canals, that's not the case. Giovanni Schiaparelli (jaw-VAHN-nee skyah-puh-REL-ee) first spotted straight lines on the planet's surface in 1877. He called those lines "canali." In Italian, canali means channels or grooves. However, people mistakenly translated the word into English as "canals." Some people even claimed Martians built the "canals." When viewed from Earth by telescopes with limited **resolution**, the canals are nothing more than optical illusions caused by craters and other surface features.

The deepest canyon on Mars is 4.35 miles (7 km) deep.

What is **Sputnik?**

Sputnik was Earth's first orbiting satellite. The Soviet Union launched Sputnik on October 4, 1957. The satellite traveled 18,000 miles (29,000 km) per hour. It took roughly 96 minutes to circle Earth. When Sputnik orbited the planet, it didn't do much—except beep. People could even watch it as it passed over head. Sputnik's launch touched off a race to the moon between the Soviet Union and the United States. Sputnik burned up in the atmosphere on January 4, 1958, as it fell from its orbit.

HAVE ANY RUSSIANS WALKED ON THE MOON?

Although the United States and the Soviet Union battled one another in the space race to the moon, only Americans have set foot on the moon. However, in 1959, the Soviet-built *Luna 2* was the first human-made spaceship to reach the lunar surface.

Sputnik was the world's first spacecraft.

WHO WAS THE FIRST WOMAN IN SPACE?

Valentina Vladimirovna Tereshkova was a Soviet cosmonaut and the first woman in space. On June 16, 1963, Tereshkova blasted into orbit, where she circled Earth 48 times. Before becoming a cosmonaut, Tereshkova was a factory worker. The first American woman in space was Sally Ride, who rode into space on June 18, 1983, aboard the space shuttle *Challenger*.

Cuba, the Soviet Union's close friend, honored Tereshkova on a postage stamp.

How were planets formed?

Our solar system, and the entire universe for that matter, started with a big bang some 13.7 billion years ago! The explosion threw out a lot of dust and gas. The explosion released so much energy that it made the dust and gas mixture cook. Bits of dust banded together, making bigger clumps. As these clumps of dust got larger, gravity held them together. In time, one clump of gas began to generate its own energy, forming our sun. The remaining dust and gas came together and swirled around the new sun. Eventually these bits of dust and gas turned into the planets.

WHY DON'T PLANETS ORBIT IN PERFECT CIRCLES?

Planets revolve around the sun in **elliptical**, or oval-like orbits, also known as eccentric orbits. The sun's gravitational pull tugs the planets one way, while the other planets tug each other in other ways. This planetary tug-of-war, along with the speed and time it takes a planet to orbit the sun, causes an eccentric orbit.

Did people once believe the sun revolved around Earth?

Everyone from the ancient Greeks up through people living in the Middle Ages, which lasted from around 400 to 1500 A.D., believed Earth was the center of the universe. They believed the sun, the moon, and the planets revolved around Earth. In 1543, an astronomer named Nicolas Copernicus said the Earth and the planets revolved around the sun. In 1610, Galileo Galilei, an Italian astronomer, used a telescope to prove that Copernicus was right.

Why aren't all planets rocky like Earth?

When the solar system first began to form, some of the dust from an exploding star joined together to form planets. Because it was so cold in the outer reaches of the solar system, some of the gas and dust froze into huge gas balls such as Jupiter and Saturn. Planets closer to the sun, such as Earth and Mars, turned into big chunks of rock.

WHY ARE THE RINGED PLANETS NEAR EACH OTHER?

Jupiter, Saturn, and Neptune have so much mass and so much gravity that they are able to hold onto their rings. If these planets were closer to the sun like the Earth, Venus, and Mercury, the sun's gravitational pull would have shredded these rings to pieces.

Why do some planets have rings?

Some planets act like a catcher's mitt. When small moons and comets get too close to a planet, gravity rips them apart. Bits of rock and ice begin orbiting the planet, eventually forming rings.

Saturn has a ring that can hold 1 billion Earths.

Why does Earth have a moon?

Scientists have scratched their heads for centuries trying to figure out where the moon came from. They believe an object about the size of Mars slammed into Earth a long time ago. That crash sent a huge chunk of Earth into outer space where it began orbiting the planet as our moon. Earth's gravitational pull keeps the moon in place.

Did Earth ever have **more than one moon?**

In the early 1980s, two scientists came up with a theory in which they said Earth once had many moons. According to this theory, Earth was struck by some huge object, sending hundreds, if not thousands, of smaller objects into space. These "moonlets" lingered between the moon and Earth for 100 million years. Then, Earth's orbit suddenly shifted. When that happened, the moonlets drifted away or crashed onto the surfaces of the moon and Earth.

WHY DID PEOPLE ONCE THINK THERE WERE SEAS ON THE MOON?

Long before telescopes and spaceships, humans viewed the moon with naked eyes. They couldn't see mountains or valleys, but they did see huge areas that they believed were seas—just like on Earth. We still call these areas seas although they are not wet.

Why is Pluto no longer considered a planet?

A planet is an object that orbits the sun with enough mass to allow gravity to form a round shape. Once upon a time, Pluto was the smallest, coldest, and least understood planet in the solar system. Many people said Pluto shouldn't be a planet at all. They said Pluto was too small and basically just a chunk of ice like many other objects in the Kuiper Belt, a disk-shaped region beyond the orbit of Neptune. In 2006, the International Astronomical Union (IAU) formally downgraded Pluto to a dwarf planet, which is smaller than a regular planet.

How long would it take a spacecraft to reach Pluto?

Pluto is roughly 2.9 billion miles from the sun. Pluto is so far away that a spacecraft would need about nine years to reach the planet from Earth. In January 2006, NASA launched the first mission to Pluto, called *New Horizons*. The unmanned spacecraft will reach its closest encounter with Pluto in July 2015. On February 25, 2010, *New Horizons* reached the half-way point between Earth and Pluto.

WHY DO HUMANS WEIGH LESS ON THE MOON THAN ON EARTH?

Since the moon is much smaller than Earth, the force of gravity is less. Gravity on the moon is about one-sixth as strong as gravity on Earth. So, humans weigh less on the moon than they do on Earth. For example, if you weighed 100 pounds (45.36 kg) on Earth, you would weigh about 16 pounds (7.6 kg) on the moon.

Why do stars form?

Stars are born in giant clouds of dust. Such clouds are scattered throughout the galaxy. Inside these clouds, gravity causes gas and dust to collapse. As that happens, the stuff in the center of the cloud heats up. The hot core at the heart of the collapsing cloud—known as a protostar—will one day become a star.

WILL THE SUN STOP SHINING SOMEDAY?

Yes, but not for at least 5 billion years. The sun is a ball of superheated gases, made up mostly of hydrogen, a small amount of helium, and very small amounts of other elements. The sun uses these gases to generate heat and light. In about 5 billion years the hydrogen in the sun will run out. When that happens, there won't be enough fuel for the sun to shine or give off heat.

What is a supernova?

Stars are born. They live out their lives, and then they explode and die. As a star begins to explode, its core quickly collapses. As the core collapses, the star releases a whole lot of energy. Such a massive amount of energy causes the star to erupt into a supernova. A supernova will shine a billion times brighter than our sun before it fades from view.

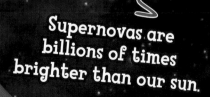

Supernovas are billions of times brighter than our sun.

Where does our solar system end?

Far beyond Neptune and Pluto is the boundary of our solar system, a place called the heliopause. The heliopause is where the sun's gravity has little effect. Beyond the heliopause lies deep space.

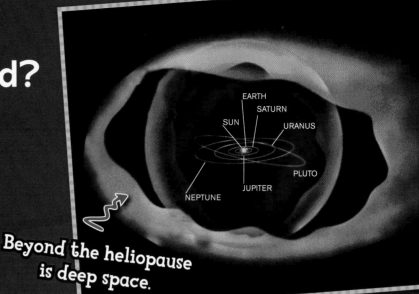

EARTH
SATURN
SUN
URANUS
PLUTO
JUPITER
NEPTUNE

Beyond the heliopause is deep space.

WHY CAN'T WE BREATHE IN SPACE?

Gravity holds everything on Earth in place, including oxygen in the atmosphere. We need oxygen in every breath to stay alive. The Earth's atmosphere provides that so we can breathe. There are a lot of gases in space, and oxygen is one of them. Because there is so little gravity in space, there's nothing to hold the gases together to create any atmosphere. Whatever gas there is spreads out very quickly over great distances, making it impossible for us to breathe without a spacesuit.

We cannot count the number of galaxies in the universe.

WHY DON'T STARS LIGHT UP THE NIGHT SKY?

Since the universe is expanding, distant stars and galaxies are moving farther away from us all the time. As that distance increases, the amount of light energy reaching Earth from the stars decreases. The farther away a star is, the less bright it will look to us. However, we won't see the night sky get any darker as the universe expands. Why? The starlight we see today is the light that left the galaxies and stars billions of years ago. Because it takes so long for a star's light to reach Earth, it would take billions of years before we would see the light of the star dim.

51

Why is our **galaxy shaped differently** than **other galaxies**?

As galaxies get older, gravity and the **centrifugal force** of spinning gas change their shapes. Galaxies contain hundreds of billions of stars. Some galaxies are spiral-shaped, some are elliptical, and some are irregular in shape. Spiral galaxies, such as our Milky Way, look like pinwheels, with outstretched arms and a bulging center. Other galaxies are shaped like cigars or sombreros.

Why can't we see the center of the **Milky Way**?

Our solar system is on the edge of the Milky Way. We can see the fuzzy band of stars that make up a portion of the Milky Way, but we cannot see the center of the galaxy with our naked eyes. There are too many stars and too much gas in the way. However special telescopes can "see" the center of the Milky Way.

WHAT GALAXIES CAN WE SEE WITHOUT TELESCOPES?

We can see two of the Milky Way's closest neighboring galaxies—the Magellanic Clouds—without the help of special instruments or telescopes. The clouds appear in the Southern Hemisphere and are named after the 16th century explorer Ferdinand Magellan.

Why are **constellations** named as they are?

The ancient Greeks, Babylonians, and Egyptians were among the most avid stargazers. Each civilization named the 88 constellations, or group of stars, for **mythological** beings. To these ancient people, some of the constellations resembled animals, people, or objects.

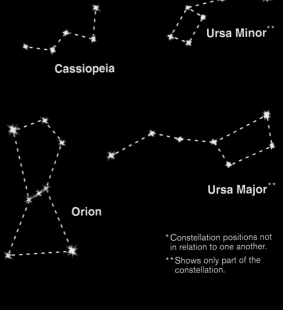

Cassiopeia

Ursa Minor**

Orion

Ursa Major**

*Constellation positions not in relation to one another.

**Shows only part of the constellation.

WHY DO THE CONSTELLATIONS MOVE ACROSS THE SKY?

It's not the constellations that are moving, but rather the Earth. Because Earth spins, we see the stars rise and set, just as we see the sun and moon rise and set.

WHY DOES THE NORTH STAR STAY IN THE SAME POSITION?

The North Star, or Polaris, sits directly above Earth's northern axis. As Earth spins, Polaris does not move from its position. For centuries, sailors have used the North Star to navigate.

What is a shooting star?

When you wish on a shooting star, you're really wishing on a meteor. Meteors are small pieces of rock or dust that smack into Earth's atmosphere with such force that **friction** causes the falling debris to burn up in a fiery display.

Most meteors are the size of pebbles.

Why are asteroids different sizes?

Asteroids are chunks of rock and metal that orbit the sun. Asteroids play a cosmic game of football because they continually smack into one another. The collisions change their shapes and sizes. The largest asteroid is Ceres, which is 580 miles (933 km) long. The smallest asteroids are a few feet in size. Some are small particles loosely bound together. Others are small pieces of solid rock.

WHAT IS THE ASTEROID BELT?

The Asteroid Belt contains hundreds of thousands of asteroids. It lies between the orbits of Jupiter and Mars. People once thought the belt formed when a planet exploded. Now, most scientists believe asteroids are bits of rock that tried to form into a planet, but never did.

Why do astronomers measure **distances** in **light years?**

Since outer space is so vast, astronomers measure distance in light years rather than miles or kilometers. A light year is the amount of time it takes light to travel (in a vacuum) in one year—roughly 5.88 trillion miles (9.46 trillion km).

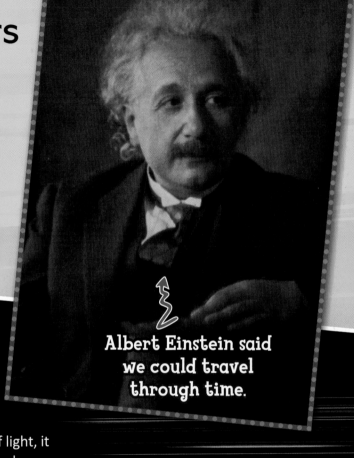

Albert Einstein said we could travel through time.

Why can't we travel at the speed of light?

If the car of the future could travel at the speed of light, it would move 186,000 miles (300,000 km) per second, or 670 million miles (1,079 million km) per hour. At that speed you would get to the moon in 1.2 seconds. Theoretically, we can travel at the speed of light, but it would take more energy than we could generate.

Why are some people taller than others?

Genes—and we're not talking blue jeans—play a leading role in people's heights. Genes are inherited characteristics such as eye and hair color. Some genes regulate our body's growth hormones, as well as how big our bones get. Moreover, in 2007, scientists found the first gene linked directly to height. They discovered that humans inherit two copies of the gene, one from each parent. Inheriting one form of the gene adds about .2 of an inch (.5 cm) to a person's height. Inheriting two forms of the same gene adds nearly .4 of an inch (1 cm). Environmental factors, diet, and overall health also help determine how tall a person grows.

Yao Ming stands 7 feet 6 inches (2.29 m) tall.

HOW DO HUMANS AGE?

Why we age has a lot to do with hormones (the chemicals that control our body functions), our health, and our diet. Diseases later in life can affect how our brain functions, including memory and personality. Even such things as whether we're married, where we live, how much money we make, and how much education we have, affect how we age.

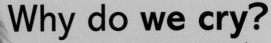

Why do **we cry?**

Grown men cry. Babies cry. We cry when we are sad, or when we are hurt. We even cry when we peel onions. Not all tears are the same, however. Sad movies or physical pain create psychic tears—tears that communicate emotions. Peeling onions creates reflex tears—tears caused by irritants in the environment.

WHY DO MY EYES GET TEARS WHEN I'M NOT CRYING?

Did you know eyes squeeze out 5 to 10 ounces (150 to 300 ml) of tears a day? In fact, your eyes are full of tears right now. Every time you blink (about once every five seconds), your eyes create basal tears. Basal tears are tears that lubricate your eyeballs to keep them clean and healthy.

Why do we get **crusty stuff** in the **corners of our eyes?**

Some people call them "eye boogers," others call them "eye snots." Whatever the term, it refers to the crusty stuff that gathers in the corners of our eyes, especially after sleeping. This "stuff," known as rheum, is thin mucus that naturally seeps from both eyes, gathering and drying in the corners. Eye mucus is made up of skin, blood cells, and dust.

Why do we need food to live?

Your body needs fuel to run. That fuel comes from nutrients. Nutrients come from food. There are six classes of nutrients found in food. They include: carbohydrates, fat, protein, vitamins, minerals, and water. By giving your body the proper amounts of nutrients and energy, you're giving yourself a better chance at staying healthy.

WHY DO SOME PEOPLE CRAVE JUNK FOOD?

Some researchers say that people can become addicted to sugar and fat—the two main ingredients in junk food. One study found that a diet high in fat changes the brain's biochemistry in the same way that some drugs do. Scientists say high-fat diets release brain chemicals called opioids. Opioids reduce the feeling of being full, so people eat more. Rats in one study loved their diets of high-fat food so much that they just kept eating. The rats also loved sugar. When sugar was taken away from them, the rats' teeth started chattering and their bodies shook.

WHY IS EXERCISE IMPORTANT?

Exercise burns calories and can keep you trim and fit. Exercise also can relax you and lessen stress. Exercise keeps your body's organs, such as the heart and lungs, healthy.

You can lose 1 pound (.45 kg) by burning 3,500 calories.

Why do people go bald?

Homer Simpson used to have a full head of hair. But every time Marge told her husband that she was going to have a baby, TV's favorite cartoon dad yanked out whatever curls he had. Luckily, most people don't go bald this way. Baldness is caused by a person's genes and hormones. Genes are inherited characteristics such as eye and hair color. Hormones control how the body functions. The actual process of going bald, however, remains a mystery—except if you're Homer Simpson. Chances are if you are a guy and your dad has gone bald, you probably will too at his age!

Why does hair turn gray?

Hair turns gray or white because we get older. Every strand of hair has a root that keeps the hair anchored in place. The root is surrounded by a follicle under the skin. Each follicle has pigment cells that produce a chemical called **melanin**. Melanin gives hair its color. As a person gets older the pigment cells die off. As that happens, each strand of hair no longer contains as much melanin. That causes the hair to turn gray or white.

WHY DO SOME PEOPLE HAVE MORE HAIR THAN OTHERS?

Some people are just downright hairy. They have hairy arms, hairy backs, and hairy legs. Genes and hormones determine whether someone can grow a lot of hair. For some, hair grows like a weed. For others, it does not. Each hair on a person's head grows from its own hair follicle at a rate of about a half an inch (13 mm) every month.

What is hay fever?

Hay fever's real name is rhinitis (rye-NEYE-tis). People who suffer from hay fever are allergic to **pollen** and other particles in the air, which affect some part of the nose. As a result, a person might have itchy, watery eyes, a stuffed nose, or a drippy throat. Dust mites, animal dander, mold spores, and fabric fibers can also cause hay fever. Nearly 15-20 percent of Americans suffer from hay fever. Roughly 10,000 children in the U.S. miss school each day because of hay fever.

Ah-choo!
Thousands of kids miss school each day because of hay fever!

WHY DOES POISON IVY MAKE ME ITCH?

Have you ever heard this rhyme: "*Leaves of three, let them be*"? When you're out in the yard or hiking in the woods, stay away from plants that have groups of three leaves growing together. Those plants could be poison ivy. The leaves of poison ivy, poison oak, and poison sumac produce a colorless, oil-like substance called **urushiol**. About 60 percent of people are allergic to urushiol. When they touch the leaves of these nasty plants, the skin becomes red and itchy.

Blisters often appear when someone comes in contact with urushiol

WHY ARE SOME PEOPLE ALLERGIC TO CERTAIN FOODS?

Food allergies are very serious. Roughly, 3.3 million people are allergic to peanuts alone. Millions more are allergic to milk, cheese, and other dairy products. Allergies develop when the body's **immune system** mistakes something usually harmless for a substance that is harmful to the body. An allergic reaction occurs when the body tries to fight off the substance.

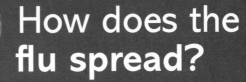

How does the flu spread?

Influenza, commonly called "the flu," is caused by viruses that infect a person's **respiratory system.** The flu spreads through sneezes and coughs. Tiny drops from a cough or sneeze can travel through the air up to three feet (. 9144 m). That flu-infected air can then be inhaled by a person, eventually causing that person to become ill. The virus can also spread when people touch the droplets that come from another person, and then touch their own mouth, nose, or eyes before washing their hands.

HOW DOES ASPIRIN CURE MY HEADACHE?

A chemical called ASA is the main ingredient in aspirin. ASA latches onto an **enzyme** in the body's cells. This enzyme creates a chemical called prostaglandin (pros-tuh-GLAN-din). Prostaglandin's job is to send messages to the brain telling it that the head is in pain. An aspirin changes the enzyme so it can no longer make prostaglandin. So, the pain messages to the brain stop, and your headache disappears. Never take an aspirin without asking for a parent's okay.

When were **antibiotics** invented?

Antibiotics are medications that kill bacteria without harming the body's cells. British scientist Sir Alexander Fleming first discovered penicillin in 1928, but it didn't gain widespread use until the 1940s, just in time to prevent infections from battlefield wounds in the final years of World War II. Penicillin has since saved millions of lives. Today, there are many types of antibiotics.

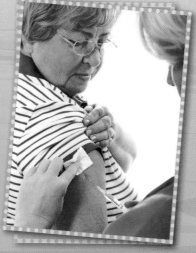

61

Why is
blood important?

Dracula isn't the only one who needs blood to survive. We all do. Blood carries nutrients to every cell in the body. Blood is a mixture of cells and plasma. Plasma is the liquid portion of blood. Red blood cells carry the oxygen your body needs to survive. Red blood cells swim in plasma, as do white blood cells, which fight infection. Plasma also carries vitamins, minerals, hormones, and other things that the body needs.

Donating blood saves lives!

Why do we bleed?

When a blood vessel is damaged, blood spews out. The bigger the hole, the faster a person bleeds. As the heart beats, it pumps blood through a system of blood vessels—elastic tubes that carry blood to every part of the body. There are three main types of blood vessels: arteries, which carry blood away from the heart to all of the body's tissues; veins, which carry blood to the heart; and capillaries, which connect arteries and veins.

WHY IS BLOOD RED?

Blood contains a protein called hemoglobin. Hemoglobin carries oxygen. When hemoglobin comes in contact with oxygen, the hemoglobin changes its color, giving blood its reddish hue. You might have noticed that the veins in your body look dark. Veins look dark because the un-oxygenated blood in them is dark.

Why does the body produce saliva?

Spit is super! Spit is good! Just don't spit on the sidewalk. Spit, otherwise known as saliva, is a clear liquid that is made in your mouth 24/7. It is made up mostly of water and other chemicals. Glands on the inside of each cheek, on the bottom of the mouth, and under the jaw near the front of the mouth, produce about 2 to 4 pints (1 to 2 L) of saliva each day. Saliva makes food moist, which makes it easier to swallow. Saliva also keeps the tongue wet so you can taste foods better. Saliva helps keep your mouth clean and breaks down food before it reaches your stomach.

Saliva helps you swallow food.

WHY DOES PUS FORM ON A CUT?

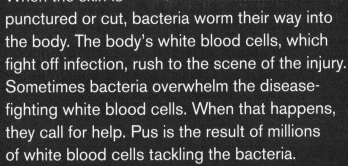

When you cut yourself, you are opening yourself up (no pun intended) to an infection. Bacteria cause infections. When the skin is punctured or cut, bacteria worm their way into the body. The body's white blood cells, which fight off infection, rush to the scene of the injury. Sometimes bacteria overwhelm the disease-fighting white blood cells. When that happens, they call for help. Pus is the result of millions of white blood cells tackling the bacteria.

Why do I cough up green stuff when I'm sick?

What you are coughing up is phlegm (flem), the sticky stuff that drips down the back of your throat when you have a cold. The respiratory system's mucus membranes produce phlegm. Viruses or bacteria will often lodge in the lungs or in some other portion of the respiratory system. When that happens, your body produces mucus to fight off the invaders. Phlegm is thicker than normal mucus. The body tries to get rid of phlegm with a cough. If phlegm cannot be expelled, it can build up and become thicker and green.

Why do I have a belly button?

While you were in your mother's womb waiting to be born, you had to eat and breathe. Of course, you couldn't order a pizza or go out for hamburgers, so nature gave you the next best thing— an umbilical cord. The umbilical cord connects a developing **embryo**, or **fetus**, with the mother's placenta, a lining that transfers blood and nutrients from the mother to the fetus. The cord's main function is to carry nourishment and oxygen from the placenta to the fetus or embryo. The cord also carries out waste material. Your belly button, or navel, is the place where your umbilical cord was attached to you before it was cut at birth.

"Chicken skin" means you're cold or scared.

WHY DO WE HAVE FINGERNAILS?

You can paint them! You can bite them! You can scratch an itch with them! Fingernails are one of the things that separate **primates**, including humans, from other mammals. Basically, fingernails are flat claws. A long time ago, primates lost their claws and developed fingernails. They used their fingernails to move about and to grasp smaller objects, such as tree branches filled with fruit. When humans evolved, we kept our fingernails. They help us perform a variety of tasks including scratching a bite, peeling a fruit, undoing a knot, and opening a package of string cheese.

Why do I get goose bumps?

You're watching a scary movie. Just before the zombie pokes its head out of the closet, you get goose bumps on your arms. Goose bumps, or chicken skin, are short-lived changes in your skin caused by cold or fear. Small muscles are attached to the tiny hairs in your skin. When you are cold or scared, the muscles contract, pulling the hair upright and causing goose bumps.

How can you stop the hiccups?

Sometimes people eat or drink so fast or get so excited that they begin to hiccup. Humans hiccup when something causes the diaphragm to spasm. The diaphragm is the large muscle that separates the thorax (the part of the body that contains the lungs and heart) from the abdomen (the part of the body that contains the stomach and intestines). This spasm causes you to take a breath which is suddenly stopped when the vocal cords close. The result is a "hiccup." But how do you stop hiccups? There's no sure way to cure them, but you can try holding your breath for 30 seconds, then exhaling gradually. You can also breathe into a paper bag five times in a row or take several gulps of water without stopping.

Holding your breath might cure the hiccups!

WHY DO I ITCH?

A mosquito bites you. *Scratch*! *Scratch*, scratch, scratch. Itching can drive a person crazy. The skin is the largest organ a person has. It covers 20 square feet (2 sq m). Skin is exposed to things that make people itch all the time, such as bug bites, poison ivy, scratches, and cuts. Itching starts with some irritation. The itch is your body's way of telling your brain that something is wrong. People automatically scratch itches in an attempt to remove the irritant.

WHY DOES A SCAB FORM ON A CUT?

Scabs form when blood cells called platelets (PLAYT-lits) rush toward a cut when the cut breaks your skin. As the clot hardens, it becomes a crusty and dark scab. Scabs are good. They help keep germs and other stuff out of the wound. That gives the skin cells a chance to heal. If you have a scab, don't pick it off. Let it fall off naturally.

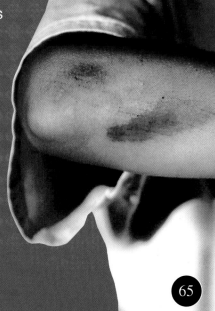

Why do we
to sleep?

Yawn! It's time for bed. Sleep is important, yet scientists don't know why. Doctors recommend that most kids spend eight hours a day, or 2,920 hours a year, sleeping. Scientists believe that muscles don't need to sleep. They just need to relax every now and again. The brain seems to need to sleep, although no one knows why. One theory suggests that sleep allows the brain to review all the bits of information people gather while awake. Another theory says brains need sleep to help bodies flush out waste. Other scientists say sleep gives people the energy needed to help do things such as ride a bike or play the trumpet.

Why do we dream?

As is true with sleep, scientists don't really know why we dream. Some researchers say dreaming serves no real purpose. Others say dreaming is important to our mental and physical health. Some doctors say dreams may be a reflection of a person's waking thoughts and wants.

WHY DOES YOUR BODY SOMETIMES "JERK" BEFORE YOU DRIFT OFF TO SLEEP?

You're about to drift off to sleep and your body suddenly jerks you awake. Scientists call this jerk a hypnic (HIP-nik) or myoclonic (my-uh-KLAH-nik) jerk. No one knows why this happens. Some scientists think the brain causes people to jerk because it gets confused when muscles start to relax. For a second, you think you're falling. Your brain tells your muscles to tense up to "catch" yourself before you fall.

Doctors say you should sleep 2,920 hours a year!

Why don't kids who are **color blind see** everything **in black and white?**

Life isn't black and white for kids who are color blind. In fact, color blind people can see most colors. When a person looks at an object, light enters the front of the eyes through the **lens**. Light then travels to the **retina**, which acts like a big movie screen. The retina is packed with cells made up of rods and cones. Rods help people see in black and white. Cones allow people to see objects in color. Each cone has a different **pigment**. These pigments allow a person to tell the difference between colors. Color blind kids might only be missing one particular type of cone, such as green or red. Although the person can see other colors, they might see gray for the cones they are missing.

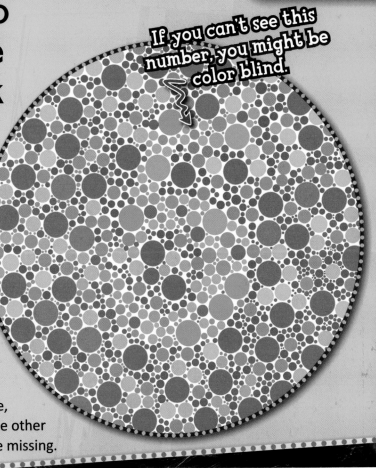

If you can't see this number, you might be color blind.

WHY DO WE BLINK?

Eyes have their own windshield washing fluid—tears. Blinking spreads tears across the eye like a windshield wiper, making sure the eyes are always clean and wet.

HOW DO EYELASHES KEEP DUST FROM GETTING INSIDE THE EYE?

Eyelashes curve up to keep water and sweat from the eye, while directing it to flow down the cheek or nose. Eye lashes also keep dust and dirt from getting into our eyes.

Why is sweat salty?

The human body is a huge salt shaker. Salt is one of the ingredients of sweat, or perspiration. When a person sweats, the body releases the watery liquid that remains after blood plasma filters out red blood cells and platelets. Plasma contains a teaspoon of salt per liter.

WHY DO WE SWEAT?

Sweating is the body's way of cooling itself off, whether a person is stressing over a big test or running around at soccer practice. Sweat comes from the 2.6 million sweat glands in the skin.

Everyone has thousands of sweat glands.

WHY DO SOME PEOPLE SWEAT MORE THAN OTHERS?

Some people who sweat a lot may have a condition called hyperhidrosis (hi-per-hi-DROH-sis). Low blood sugar and some diseases might cause excessive sweating. Medicines might also make some people sweat a lot.

Why does sweat smell?

Sweat stinks. The smell comes from bacteria that live on skin. These tiny creatures mix with sweat causing a foul odor. So please wash up after you exercise—for all our sakes.

Why does my nose run?

Is your nose running? Shut the door before it runs out of the house. Okay, bad joke, but many people do get runny noses. A runny nose, also known as rhinorrhea (ri-nuh-REE-uh), occurs when tissue and blood vessels inside the nose are swollen with too much fluid or mucus. Allergies, colds, the flu, dust, and even spicy foods can make your nose run.

It's not a good idea to pick your nose.

WHY DOES EVERYONE GET SNOT?

Snot and boogers are just two names we give nasal mucus. Think of the nose as a vacuum cleaner, sucking in bits of dirt and dust each day. Nose hair traps that dirt and dust. Mucus surrounds the dirt, forming slimy lumps before it gets into the lungs. When people blow or—*yuck!*—pick their noses, they remove all that junk from their noses.

Why do I have ear wax?

Ear wax isn't used to make candles, but it does help the body defend itself against unwanted invaders. Ear wax traps dirt and bacteria that would otherwise get into the ears. Too much ear wax can be a problem if it hardens.

Why does my stomach growl after I eat?

Everything is quiet and suddenly—*growwwwwwwwwwwwwllIIIIII*—someone's stomach starts making a grumbling, rumbling, or sloshing noise. When Winnie the Pooh says that there's a "rumbly in my tumbly," he's trying to say the muscles in his digestive system are moving and pushing a gooey mixture of food and liquid, known as chyme (kīm), through his **digestive tract**. Moving along with the mush is air and gas, which gets squeezed, creating the noises you hear.

The smell of flatulence comes from bacteria.

Why do I pass gas?

Everybody—from best friends to teachers—passes gas. The average person passes gas 14 times a day. Gas forms in the digestive tract and is made up of carbon dioxide, oxygen, nitrogen, and other gases. We get gas because we swallow small bits of air as we eat or drink. Gas also forms when the body does not digest certain foods. Then, the body expels gas through burping or passing it through the **rectum** as flatulence.

WHY DOES FLATULENCE SMELL BAD?

The smell comes from bacteria in the large intestine that release small amounts of gas containing sulfur.

People with light skin often get freckles.

Why do some kids have freckles?

Freckles are batches of skin cells that contain color. Some of these cells are tan colored; others are light brown and very small. Most kids who have freckles have light complexions. People with light or fair complexions have less melanin (MEL-uh-nin) in their skin. Melanin is a chemical that protects the skin from the sun's ultraviolet rays, which cause freckles. People with fair skin are more likely to get freckles than people with darker skin.

Why do some kids have birthmarks?

Birthmarks are marks on the skin. People get birthmarks at, well, birth. There are several types of birthmarks. One, known as a **hemangioma** (hem-an-gi-O-ma) occurs when tiny blood vessels grow in one area on the skin. A strawberry hemangioma looks like a tiny strawberry. Most strawberry hemangiomas go away. Another type of birthmark is a port wine stain, which is either purple or maroon in color.

WHAT ARE MOLES ON A PERSON'S SKIN?

Moles are a collection of cells that contain color. People often refer to them as beauty marks. Moles are not painful.

What happens
when I sneeze?

Ah-choo! A sneeze is another way for the body to get rid of **viruses**, bacteria, dust, dirt, hair, and other pollutants. A sneeze begins when the upper portion of the nasal lining is irritated by a virus or a bit of dust. Tiny nerves then send a signal, telling the brain that something isn't right. The brain orders the muscles in the chest and throat to contract, or tighten. The brain then tells the eyes to shut and the **palate** to close. *Ah-choo*! Chest and throat contractions make you sneeze. Sneezes can travel up to 100 miles (160.93 km) an hour, while sending 5,000 bacteria-filled water drops into the air.

It's impossible to sneeze with your eyes open!

Why do people cough?

Coughing is another way for the body to clear its respiratory system of bacteria, viruses, and other things. A cough begins when something irritates the nerves in the lungs. Mucus in the lungs traps the tiny irritants. When that happens, tiny air tubes called bronchi contract. The lungs then send a signal to the brain's cough center, telling the brain it needs to get rid of these invaders. The brain tells the glottis—two flaps of muscle that make up part of the voice box—to close. Pressure increases in the lower part of the glottis as muscles in the chest contract. The glottis reopens, and the lungs forcefully expel the air through the mouth—a cough.

Why do I feel pain when I stub my toe?

Stub a toe—*ouch*! Hit a thumb with a hammer—*ouch, ouch, ouch*! Touch a hot stove—*that hurts*! While no one likes to be in pain, pain is the body's way of telling the brain that something might be wrong. Pain travels to and from the brain along the spinal cord and nerves. Nerve cells beneath the skin sense pain. When there is an injury to the body, such as banging an elbow very hard, these tiny cells send messages to the brain, telling it that the body has been hurt.

WHY DOES A PERSON GET TIRED IN THE AFTERNOON?

A person's biological clock, known as the circadian cycle, is ticking and is responsible for afternoon sleepiness. This biological clock is affected by several things, including the release of a hormone called melatonin (mel-uh-TOE-nin). Melatonin causes sleepiness. Normally, melatonin levels rise in the mid-to-late evening and remain high for most of the night. By the time a person wakes up, the level has dropped. Many people, however, get sleepy at around 3 P. M. because their bodies release a lot of melatonin at that time.

What is a **fever**?

Fevers are good. They are our body's natural response to fighting germs. A fever occurs when an army of white blood cells battles the germs. The faster the white blood cells attack, the hotter the body gets. Not everyone has a normal temperature of 98.6°F (37°C). Some are higher, and some are lower, and these variations are fine. When the body's temperature rises beyond that, it becomes a condition known as fever. There are several reasons why people get fevers. They could have infections caused by viruses, or they could sustain an injury, such as a heart attack, heat stroke, or burn.

Why can we hear sound and see light?

Sounds are tiny vibrations, or air pressure changes, that travel as waves. These waves hit a person's eardrum. The ear then sends a signal to the brain that allows a person to hear a sound. Light is made up of tiny particles called **photons**. Photons also travel in waves reaching the eyes, which allow people to see.

Why are some sounds loud and shrill?

We hear loud and shrill sounds because there are differences in **pitch** caused by different spaces between sound waves. The closer together the waves are, the higher the sound. Sound waves are measured in **wavelengths**. The loudness of a sound is measured in decibels. At 130 decibels, a jackhammer makes a painful sound. A subway whizzes by you at an extremely loud 90 decibels.

WHY CAN DOGS HEAR BETTER THAN HUMANS?

Dogs can hear sounds at a much higher frequency than humans. Frequency is the number of times a sound wave vibrates in a second. Humans can only hear sounds within a limited range of frequency. Sometimes the frequency of a sound is so high that humans can't hear the sound, but dogs can.

Why do some older people have long ear hair?

If you are a young male, the last thing you worry about is the length of your ear hair. Like nose hair, the tiny hairs in a person's ears protect the body from dust and dirt. As a person gets older, ear hair tends to grow... and grow... and grow. No one knows why this happens. Some say a person's genes play a role in ear-hair growth. Others say hormones, or chemicals that control the activity of certain cells and organs, are the reason that some people have lots of ear hair.

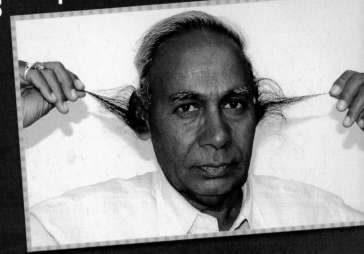

Most warts disappear on their own.

WHAT IS THE WHITE GOO THAT COMES OUT OF A POPPED PIMPLE?

The white goo is a mixture of dirt, oil, white blood cells, and bacteria. Never squeeze a pimple, because it can leave a scar.

WHY DO WARTS FORM?

A person can't get a wart from touching a frog, but a person can get a wart by becoming infected with a virus. Warts are growths on the skin caused by the human papillomavirus (PAP-uh-loh-mah-vi-rus) also known as HPV. Some warts appear on the hands and fingers. Others grow on the underside of the feet. Some warts are bumpy and rough. Others are smooth and flat. Some are yellow. Some are brown. Some are skin-colored.

WHY DOES FOOD SOMETIMES TASTE BAD TO SOMEONE WITH A STUFFED UP NOSE?

The nose's sense of smell and the mouth's taste buds work together when people eat. The taste buds sense the taste of food (salty, bitter, sour, sweet). The nose detects specific odors. When a person chews food, the person senses the food's odor with the nose's olfactory (smell) receptors, located behind the bridge of the nose. If the nose is stuffed, the receptors won't work as well and food won't taste as good.

Why do humans have fingerprints?

The series of lines, ridges, loops, and curves on the tips of your fingers are your fingerprints. Each person has a unique fingerprint. Genes play a part in the development of human fingerprints. However, when a baby is inside its mother's womb, it doesn't have any prints. Fingerprints develop as the baby presses against the inside of the womb. That's why identical twins have different fingerprints.

WHY DO PEOPLE GET THIRSTY?

People get thirsty because they lose more water than they drink. When your body needs water, it will let you know. Thirst receptors in the back of the throat dry up, which sends a message to the brain, telling a person to drink.

Why are people ticklish?

When someone tickles you, they are stimulating the delicate nerve endings just under the skin. Some parts of our body are more ticklish than others. Feet are especially sensitive to tickling because feet have large nerve endings.

WHY DON'T WE LAUGH WHEN WE TICKLE OURSELVES?

Try it. Not much happens, right? You might think you would feel the same sensation as if someone else was tickling you. Not so. Scientists don't know why we can't tickle ourselves. Some suspect that the element of surprise has a lot to do with it. When we tickle ourselves, we have lost the surprise. Our brain—specifically the **cerebellum**—knows what is happening and that there's no reason to laugh.

Why can we whistle?

People can whistle while they work, or they can whistle to call the dog. People whistle in the dark, and some whistle for fun. Whistling is a sound produced by controlling a stream of air flowing through a small hole. Most people whistle by pursing their lips together and blowing. Others can whistle through their fingers or cupped hands. People whistle to attract attention, to show approval or disapproval, or to play a song.

WHY ARE LIPS RED?

Lips are red because blood vessels known as capillaries are located near the thin skin of your lips.

Why does it hurt to bite on aluminum foil?

Biting on foil might cause a sharp pain. That pain is a weak electric shock. When people with metal fillings in their teeth bite down on a piece of foil, the acid from the mouth's saliva turns the mouth into a battery. When teeth chomp down on foil, they receive an electric current that passes through the fillings into the sensitive part of the teeth. We don't recommend trying this!

Why do knuckles crack?

Knuckles are joints in the fingers where two separate bones meet. All of the body's joints are surrounded by a case of thick, clear liquid that keeps the **cartilage**, tissues, and muscles lubricated and nourished. Gases, such as oxygen, nitrogen, and carbon dioxide, float inside the liquid. When you bend your fingers, you stretch the case around the joint. That increases the amount of fluid. When that happens, the bubbles in the fluid begin to burst, producing a pop.

WHY DO OUR EYES TWITCH?

Eye twitching is really annoying. It can happen when you're reading a book or talking to a friend. Researchers say eye twitching is caused by muscle spasms in the eyelid. These spasms may be brought on by stress or physical eye strain.

Eyes twitch when muscles in the eyelid spasm!

Why is some hair curly?

Hair is protein. Protein contains sulfur atoms called sulfides. When two sulfur atoms come together they form a disulfide bond. The protein bends when that bonding takes place. The more disulfide bonds there are, the curlier the hair will be. People with straight hair will often curl their hair by using chemicals to create many disulfide bonds.

Why is the London Bridge
in Arizona?

The old nursery rhyme goes like this: "London Bridge is falling down, falling down, falling down..." In the late 1960s, that's exactly what was happening. Built in 1831, the London Bridge spanned the Thames River in London, England. By the late 1960s, the bridge was in disrepair, sinking under its own weight into the clay of the Thames. That's when Robert McCulloch bought the bridge for $2.4 million. In 1967, he moved the bridge brick-by-brick to Lake Havasu City, Arizona. By 1971, London Bridge was once again opened—this time in the U.S.

The famed Londo Bridge was rebu in Arizona.

WHY IS VENICE SINKING?

For centuries, flooding has been a problem for those living in Venice, Italy, a series of islands in the Adriatic Sea. During high tides, water spills over the city's seawalls, flooding the city even more. Between 1950 and 1970, Venice sank 5 inches (12.70 cm) because engineers pumped water from under the city for use in factories on Italy's mainland. The pumping caused the seabed and buildings to sink. Venice continues to sink today.

WHY IS THE TOWER OF PISA LEANING?

Long before workers completed the third floor of the Tower of Pisa, the marble structure began tilting. The problem started when engineer Bonanno Pisano designed the 185-foot-tall (56.39 m) tower with a stone foundation that was only 10 feet (3.05 m) thick. The construction site was also very soft. Between the weak foundation and soft soil, the 16,000-ton (14.515 MT) structure tilted. To make up for this, the builders made each new floor a bit taller on the side closest to the ground. That made the tower lean in the other direction. Recently, engineers worked on the tower to give its unusual structure greater strength.

Why is an area in Beijing, China, called the Forbidden City?

Located in the middle of Beijing, China, the Forbidden City was once the imperial palace of Ming Dynasty rulers. For more than 500 years, the city, built between 1406 and 1420, served as the emperor's home and the political and ceremonial center of the country. The area, with its 800 buildings, was called the Forbidden City because only China's royal family could live there. Today, the Forbidden City is a popular tourist spot.

People are no longer forbidden in China's Forbidden City.

WHY ARE SO MANY PRODUCTS MADE IN CHINA?

From sneakers to toys, China makes just about every kind of product. In fact, China is the world's largest economy. The country manufactures and ships goods all over the world. One reason: The Chinese don't pay their workers much money. This makes it possible to produce cheaper (but not always superior) goods.

Can you see the Great Wall of China from outer space?

When astronauts orbit Earth they can see the Great Wall of China, but they generally need a powerful telescope. Built about 2,500 years ago, the Great Wall of China is 4,163 miles (6,700 km) long. NASA scientists say the Great Wall is often hard to see and photograph because its color blends in with the surrounding area.

Astronauts really can see the Great Wall of China from outer space!

Why did the Chinese build the Great Wall?

The Great Wall of China is actually a series of separate walls in the northern part of the country that the Chinese eventually linked. They built the wall to defend against attacks. An army of peasants, soldiers, slaves, and prisoners built the Great Wall. The wall stretches from Bo Hai Bay, on the eastern coast, to Gansu Province, in the western desert.

HOW LONG DID IT TAKE TO BUILD THE GREAT WALL OF CHINA?

It took several hundred years to build the Great Wall of China. The first section of the Great Wall was built in the 7th century B.C. In 221 B.C., the first emperor of the Qin Dynasty ordered that all the walls be joined. The Chinese built much of the wall by pounding earth between board frames.

What is the Chunnel?

Not long ago, the only way people could travel between France and England was by boat or by airplane. The two countries are separated by a body of water called the English Channel. In 1994, workers finished building a rail tunnel—nicknamed the Chunnel (a combination of "Channel" and "tunnel")—under the Channel, connecting the two countries. The 31-mile (50-km) tunnel makes traveling between the two countries easier as travelers ride a high-speed passenger train.

WHAT IS THE LARGEST DAM IN THE WORLD?

At 7,575 feet (2,309 m), the Three Gorges Dam in China is the largest dam in the world. The Three Gorges Dam spans the Yangtze River, holding back enough water to create a huge lake nearly 410 miles (660 km) long. Much like Hoover Dam in the U.S., the Three Gorges Dam generates electricity.

WHY DOES THE GOLDEN GATE BRIDGE SWAY IN THE WIND?

The bridge across San Francisco Bay in California was built to withstand earthquakes and high winds. When builder Joseph Strauss designed the bridge's center span (the distance between the bridge towers), he made sure the roadway swayed just a bit so the bridge would not collapse when the wind blew or the Earth shook. The Golden Gate Bridge can swing sideways up to 27 feet (8.23 m).

It took four years to build the Golden Gate Bridge!

83

Why is the Statue of Liberty green?

The Statue of Liberty, which stands in New York Harbor, has always been a little green around the gills. The outer layer of the statue is made of copper. The copper reacts with wind, saltwater from the ocean, and other elements including acid rain to produce copper salts. The salts give Lady Liberty her greenish tinge.

You have to climb 154 steps to get to the head of the Statue of Liberty.

WHY DID THE FRENCH GIVE THE STATUE OF LIBERTY TO THE U.S.?

At 151 feet (46.02 m), the Statue of Liberty is the tallest woman in the world. The French gave the statue to the people of America as a sign of friendship, which the two nations forged during the American Revolution (1775-1783). The statue is a universal symbol of freedom and democracy. French sculptor, Frederic-Auguste Bartholdi, was asked to design the statue, which was dedicated on October 28, 1886, and restored in 1986.

Why is the Statue of Liberty holding a torch?

The original name of the Statue of Liberty is Liberty Enlightening the World. Frederic-Auguste Bartholdi designed the statue with a torch raised high in her right hand. The torch stands for the promise of America as a light of hope for the world. The torch also allows the Statue of Liberty to be used as a lighthouse.

WHAT WAS THE FIRST CAPITAL OF THE UNITED STATES?

The government called New York City its home from 1785 to 1790. The capital then moved to Philadelphia. By 1790, the U.S. Congress was looking for a permanent home. Members of Congress from the North and South argued over where that home should be. Finally, lawmakers settled on a plot of swampy land on the northern bank of the Potomac River that George Washington helped choose. Can you guess that city's name?

Why is the White House called the White House?

Long before the White House was the White House, it was called the President's House, the President's Mansion, or the Executive Mansion. According to legend, the White House got its name in 1811 when a coat of white paint was applied to its exterior. However, it was President Theodore Roosevelt who officially called the mansion the White House in 1901, when he had the name printed on his stationery.

It cost $23,796.82 in the 1860s to sculpt the Statue of Freedom.

What statue is on top of the U.S. Capitol?

The U.S. Capitol in Washington, D.C., is home to the U.S. Congress. Gracing the top of the Capitol's majestic dome is the bronze Statue of Freedom. The statue was designed by Thomas Crawford. The Statue of Freedom is a woman holding the shield of the United States with 13 stripes to celebrate the original 13 colonies.

85

Why didn't **George Washington** live in the White House?

Although George Washington helped pick the spot where the White House, or Executive Mansion, would be built, he never lived at that famous address. By the time the White House was completed, he had retired from the presidency. The cornerstone of the house was laid on October 13, 1792. Eight years later, President John Adams moved into the house. At the time, the building's paint and plaster were still drying. When Abigail Adams, the President's wife, arrived, she had to hang the laundry in what would become known as the East Room. Adams and his wife did not live long at that address, however. Thomas Jefferson was the second President to live in the White House, moving to the mansion in 1801.

Why was the White House built by slaves?

Slaves helped build the White House and the U.S. Capitol. Slave labor was cheap. The builders did not have to pay slaves. At the time, slavery in the South was legal. In addition, there were many slaves in Washington, D.C., because the city was a center for the Southern slave trade. Many of the builders brought their own personal slaves with them to work on the job. They also contracted with plantation owners around the city to use their slaves.

WHY DID DOLLY MADISON SAVE A PORTRAIT OF GEORGE WASHINGTON FROM A FIRE?

In 1814, Great Britain and the United States were still fighting the War of 1812. In August 1814, the British army was marching toward Washington. On August 24, the Americans lost a battle with the British a few miles from the capital city. With Washington, D.C. the next target, Dolly Madison, the wife of President James Madison, fled the White House by carriage, taking a full-length portrait of George Washington with her because Washington was an important figure in the new nation's history. That evening, the British marched into the city and set many buildings, including the White House, on fire.

Dolly Madison

Why are some deserts increasing in size?

Every year, on every continent, deserts are increasing in size—a process known as desertification. Bad farming techniques, the overgrazing of grassland by livestock, the destruction of forests by humans, droughts, and the overuse of soil all contribute to desertification. Researchers estimate that the expanding deserts affect some 200 million people living mostly in Africa, India, and South America. This has caused millions to leave their homes and lose their livelihoods.

WHY DOES FARMING CAUSE DESERTS TO FORM IN SOME PLACES?

People who farm in areas where the soil is poor and the climate dry often destroy native grasses and plants when they plow fields for crops. They also cut down trees so cattle and other livestock can graze. With no plants or trees to anchor the soil, wind and rain can wipe away topsoil, causing deserts to form.

WHAT IS THE LARGEST DESERT IN THE UNITED STATES?

Centered in Nevada, the Great Basin Desert is the largest desert in the U.S. It stretches into parts of California, Oregon, Idaho, and Utah. The desert covers about 190,000 square miles (305,775.36 sq. km).

Why does the **South American** country of Bolivia have two capitals?

What's the capital of Bolivia? If you said La Paz, you'd be right. If you said Sucre, you would be right, too. When Bolivia gained its independence from Spain in 1825, Sucre became the new nation's capital. In 1899, Bolivia had a period of political problems and many wanted the country's capital moved to La Paz. Many others disagreed. Eventually Bolivian politicians reached a compromise. La Paz became the seat of the **executive** and **legislative** branches of government, while Sucre remained home to the **judicial** branch.

Why is Easter Island called Easter Island?

The island, located in the Pacific Ocean about 2,300 miles (3,701 km) off the coast of Chile, got its name because a Dutch admiral landed there on Easter Day in 1722. Can you guess why Christmas Island in Australia is called Christmas Island?

WHY DO BRAZILIANS SPEAK PORTUGUESE INSTEAD OF SPANISH?

Although most of South America was colonized by the Spanish, the Portuguese colonized Brazil in the 1500s. At the time, most Brazilians spoke a language called Tupi. The Portuguese banned Tupi in the mid-1700s. Brazilians who speak Portuguese have mixed many Tupi words into their language.

Why do people call Australia "The Land Down Under"?

G'day, Mate! Welcome to the land down under! Many people refer to Australia as the "land down under" because it is one of only two continents entirely located south of the equator. Can you guess what the other continent is?

No part of Australia is more than 621 miles (1,000 km) from the ocean.

Was Australia really a prison?

Yes, Australia was founded as a giant prison, also known as a penal colony. In 1788, England sent its first shipload of prisoners to Australia to ease overcrowding in British prisons. The first ships of convicts landed at Botany Bay in New South Wales. Two more convict fleets reached the continent in 1790 and 1791. Although the first prisoners settled in Botany Bay, by the early 1800s convicts had settled in other locations. The prisoners worked as brick makers, carpenters, nurses, and farmers.

Australia's first aboriginal settlers came from Indonesia.

WHO ARE ABORIGINES?

Aborigines are native Australians who migrated to the continent about 40,000 years ago. Each aborigine community has its own culture, customs, and language, much like Native Americans.

89

What is the deepest point on Earth?

The deepest site on the planet is the Mariana Trench, which is 36,201 feet (11,033 m) deep. The trench is located in the Pacific Ocean near the Mariana Islands, southeast of Japan. The reason the trench is so deep has to do with **plate tectonics**. Earth's crust is made up of moving plates, floating on the molten magma of the mantle. As the magma rises through cracks in the crust, it pushes the pieces of crust apart. In some areas, the magma forces chunks of crust together. In other areas, the ocean's crust pushes beneath Earth's crust, creating deep trenches like the Mariana.

China
Japan
Philippines
Guam
Mariana Trench
Indonesia
Papua New Guinea
Australia

The Mariana Trench is the deepest point on Earth.

WHY CAN'T PEOPLE DIVE TO THE BOTTOM OF THE MARIANA TRENCH?

If you were to dive to the very bottom of the Mariana Trench, you would be squished like a bug. The pressure at the trench's deepest point is 8 tons (7,252 kg) per square inch.

Angler fish

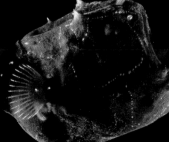

DO FISH LIVE IN THE MARIANA TRENCH?

Humans might not be able to survive at the bottom of the Mariana Trench, but hundreds of species of fish can. Species such as the angler fish and "vent crabs" thrive in the deep waters of the trench. One mud sample taken by researchers found nearly 200 different microorganisms. Not only do many animals survive in the waters of the trench, but many live for more than 100 years.

Why is Niagara Falls so large?

Niagara Falls, which borders Ontario, Canada, and New York State, began to form some 13,000 years ago as huge ice sheets carved out the Great Lakes. As Earth warmed and the ice retreated northward, melting water began to flow through present-day Lake Erie, the Niagara River, Lake Ontario, and the St. Lawrence River. Over time, rushing water created the falls from the surrounding rock. Niagara Falls is actually two falls in one, the American Falls and the Canadian or Horseshoe Falls. The American Falls is 1,060 feet (323.09 m) wide and 176 feet (53.64 m) high. The Canadian Falls is 2,600 feet (792.48 m) wide and 167 feet (50.90 m) high.

Why doesn't Niagara Falls freeze in winter?

With 150,000 gallons of water going over the falls every second, it's nearly impossible for Niagara Falls or the Niagara River to freeze over. However, an ice bridge often forms at the base of the falls and over a part of the Niagara River below the falls.

HAS ANYONE EVER TRIED TO GO OVER NIAGARA FALLS?

Since 1901, daredevils have attempted the famous stunt of trying to ride over Niagara Falls in a barrel or some other container. Annie Taylor was the first to do it and survive to talk about it. Others have gone over the falls in ball-shaped canisters, a jet ski, and steel barrels. Some have also walked across parts of the Niagara River near the falls on tightropes. About 15 people have gone over the falls in some sort of equipment. Five have died.

Why do people call Chicago "the Windy City"?

There are many theories about why Chicago is nicknamed "the Windy City." Some suspect it has to do with the "wind," or lots of talk, by the city's politicians, or the people who bragged about rebuilding Chicago after a fire in 1871 destroyed much of the town. Others say Chicago got its nickname because it is such a windy place. The *Chicago Tribune* newspaper first used the term during the early 1880s, as a way to promote the city as a summer resort with cooling breezes coming off Lake Michigan.

WHY IS NEW YORK CITY'S NICKNAME "THE BIG APPLE"?

There aren't that many apple trees in New York City, but there are many theories on how the city got its nickname, "the Big Apple." Some say sportswriter John J. Fitzgerald coined the term in the 1920s on a trip to New Orleans. Fitzgerald heard stable hands call New York's horse racing scene "the big apple." Fitzgerald returned to New York and named his horse-racing column "Notes from Around the Big Apple." The name supposedly stuck. Another story says that jazz musicians called their paying gigs "apples." The biggest "apple" of them all was to play in a New York City nightclub.

HOW DID NEW ORLEANS GET THE NICKNAME "THE BIG EASY"?

Some people claim New Orleans got its nickname "the Big Easy" because musicians could easily make money there. Others say New Orleans became "the Big Easy" because it was easy to drink alcoholic beverages there during Prohibition (1920–1933)—a time when it was illegal to buy and sell alcohol.

More than 8 million people live in the Big Apple.

Why did the ancient Egyptians build the Great Pyramid?

It is probably the grandest ancient building in the world—the Great Pyramid of Giza. Built from more than 2 million limestone blocks ranging in weight from 2.5 tons (2,268 kg) to 9 tons (8,165 kg), the 4,500-year-old pyramid was built as a tomb for King Khufu. Inside the pyramids and other tombs, the ancient Egyptians placed gold, sculptures, furniture, and other treasure that the king might need in the afterlife. They built pyramids because the shape was considered sacred.

WHY DID THE EGYPTIANS MUMMIFY THE DEAD?

In ancient Egypt, the bodies of dead rulers were preserved in a process that turned their bodies into mummies. The Egyptians believed the dead needed their bodies for the trip to the afterlife, so they carefully prepared the bodies for the journey. They placed the body's organs in special jars. They also preserved certain animals and household pets to be buried alongside the human mummy.

HOW DID ANCIENT EGYPTIANS MUMMIFY THE DEAD?

Researchers today believe that, after removing the person's lungs, stomach, and intestines through a hole in the body, and removing the brain through the nose, priests used a special salt to dry out the body. They packed the skull with salt and plaster, removing the dead person's real eyes and replacing them with artificial ones. Then they wrapped the body in linen treated with a special solution.

The Great Sphinx of Giza is half man, half lion, and stands 66.34 feet (20.22 m) high.

93

Why does planting a tree help the environment?

Breathe in. Now exhale. Everyone can thank the world's trees for those deep breaths. Planting trees helps improve the quality of the air we breathe by cleaning the atmosphere of carbon dioxide. When trees breathe in carbon dioxide, they exhale oxygen, which humans and animals need to live.

WHAT IS ONE REASON RAINFORESTS ARE IN DANGER?

One of the worst **ecological** disasters is taking place as you read this. In the world's rainforests, located mostly in South America and Asia, humans are cutting down and burning trees that soak up the **greenhouse gas** carbon dioxide. Greenhouse gases trap heat close to Earth's surface. The result is global warming, an increase in Earth's temperature. According to the Rainforest Action Network, humans cut down an area of rainforest about the size of a football field every second. This is known as clear cutting. With fewer trees, there is more carbon dioxide in the atmosphere. Clear cutting also destroys the habitat of thousands of animals.

A football field-sized chunk of the rainforest is cut down every second!

WHY ARE HUMANS BLAMED FOR POLLUTION?

Every time people turn on lights, ride in cars, or fly in planes, they are contributing to air **pollution**. Air pollution is the result of harmful air-borne substances, such as smoke from factories and electric plants, that can damage the environment and the health of humans and animals. Pollutants come in two main forms: gases and **particulates**. Gases are created when we burn **fossil fuels**, such as oil, natural gas, and coal. Particulates are tiny solid particles that automobiles pump into the atmosphere.

Why did the French build the Eiffel Tower?

Looming over Paris, France, is the Eiffel Tower, built for the World's Fair in 1889. Designed and built by Gustave Eiffel, the tower rises 1,063 feet (324 m) above the City of Light, almost twice as high as the Washington Monument.

Workers used 60 tons (54.4 MT) of paint to paint the Eiffel Tower.

WHY IS THE PARTHENON AN OPTICAL ILLUSION?

The ancient Greeks built the temple on top of a hill in Athens almost 2,500 years ago, wanting it to look perfect. To accomplish that goal, the ancient engineers needed to correct an optical illusion by creating one of their own. When seen against the sky, a straight column looks as if it gets narrow in the middle. To correct this illusion, the Greeks designed each of the outside columns with a slight bend. All lean inward, creating a picture of symmetry and straightness. If you cut the building in half, one side of the Parthenon would look the same as the other side.

WHY DID PEOPLE WANT TO BUILD A CANAL IN PANAMA?

For centuries, ships had to travel around South America to get from the Atlantic Ocean to the Pacific Ocean and back. It was a dangerous and expensive journey. Many people wanted to build a canal through Panama to connect both oceans because Panama was such a narrow strip of land. The French were the first to try, but their attempt failed in 1889. The United States then took over the project. Construction began in 1904. The work was so hard that an estimated 25,000 people died during 10 years of construction. The total cost was $375 million.

Why do countries each have a flag?

Each of the world's nations, from the tiniest to the mightiest, has a flag. Flags represent a nation and its people. A flag shows that the people are proud of their country. Some colors represent more than an historical event, they represent qualities or characteristics of a nation.

Crowns are often made with jewels.

Why do kings and queens wear crowns?

Beauty pageant winners aren't the only people who get to wear crowns. Kings and queens have been wearing crowns for centuries. They wear them as a symbol of power, wealth, and honor. Crowns are usually fashioned out of gold and jewels. No one knows when the first crown appeared.

Who was Mohandas Gandhi?

Mohandas Gandhi (GHAN-dhee) was a lawyer who fought for India's independence from Great Britain during the 1930s and 1940s. Gandhi and his followers protested in nonviolent ways. One of those ways was to stage hunger strikes. Gandhi's most famous hunger strike came in 1932 when the British put him in jail for protesting the British government's decision to separate India's electoral system by **caste**. He fasted for six days until the British reversed the decision. Gandhi's nonviolence inspired his people and millions worldwide. As India inched towards independence, Gandhi's influence grew. He used hunger strikes as a way to win concessions from the British.

Martin Luther King, Jr., entered college when he was 15.

HOW WERE SLAVES FREED DURING THE CIVIL WAR?

President Abraham Lincoln freed the slaves two years after the Civil War began. The Civil War, between the North and South, began in 1861. The South wanted to break from the Union because southerners did not want to end slavery. In 1863, Lincoln drafted the Emancipation Proclamation, which freed the slaves in the southern states. The Emancipation Proclamation also opened the way for blacks to join the Union army and abolish slavery forever.

HOW DID MARTIN LUTHER KING, JR. INSPIRE SO MANY PEOPLE?

As with Gandhi, Martin Luther King, Jr., a Baptist minister, used nonviolence to fight for civil rights for African Americans. King and his followers marched, protested, and staged **sit-ins** throughout the South during the 1960s hoping to make life better for millions of Americans. In 1963, King led his March on Washington and delivered his famous "I Have a Dream" speech in front of thousands of people. The march was credited with helping to pass the Civil Rights Act of 1964, which outlawed racial segregation in many places.

Why were the ancient Romans so powerful?

Ancient Rome was one of the mightiest civilizations on the planet. From about 31 B.C. to 476 A.D., Rome controlled most of the known world, including much of Europe, the Balkans, and the Mediterranean region. Rome became so powerful because its mighty army conquered these lands.

What were Roman families like?

Roman families included parents, children, and slaves. Generally, the father ruled the household. The average Roman family had five or six kids. Wealthy Roman families sent their children to school, while those with less money did not. In most households, boys and girls worked long hours in the fields.

Julius Caesar created a "newspaper" to let everyone know what Rome's leaders were doing.

WHO WAS JULIUS CAESAR?

Julius Caesar was a Roman politician and general who helped to transform Rome into the center of a great empire. He reformed Roman society and was proclaimed "dictator in perpetuity [forever]." A group of Roman senators, led by Marcus Junius Brutus, killed Caesar in 44 B.C., hoping to restore the Roman republic.

What destroyed the ancient city of Pompeii?

On August 24, 79 A.D., an eerie darkness covered the Italian countryside when Vesuvius, a 4,200-foot-high (1,280.16 m) volcano, blew its top. Soon, boiling mud and lava poured down the side of the mountain burning everything in its path. Thousands in the nearby cities of Pompeii and Herculaneum raced to the sea to escape fiery death. Thousands more could not outrun the ash and lava. The city was destroyed.

WHY ARE SOME PEOPLE STILL AFRAID OF VESUVIUS?

Over the centuries, Mount Vesuvius has erupted with tremendous force, and many people are still afraid it will blow again. The next eruption could have serious consequences. About 600,000 people live in 18 towns in the so called *la zona rossa*, or "the red zone" close to Vesuvius. Scientists say during the first 15 minutes of an eruption, anything within a 4 mile (6.44 km) radius could be destroyed, including many towns in the red zone.

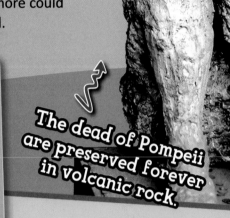

The dead of Pompeii are preserved forever in volcanic rock.

WHY IS THE ANCIENT CITY OF POMPEII SO WELL PRESERVED?

When Vesuvius was done spitting lava and ash on that awful day in 79 A.D., the eruption had blanketed Pompeii and other cities under a blanket of ash and mud, preserving the city forever. Scientists encased the remains of those caught in the eruption in concrete after molds of the bodies were left in the hardening ash and mud.

Why did the Maya build pyramids?

Deep within the jungles of Mexico and Central America, the Maya, a Native American civilization, built amazing pyramids. The Maya began building pyramids mostly for religious purposes some 3,000 years ago. Some pyramids had stairs so people could climb to the top and hold sacrificial **rituals**. The Maya built the pyramids taller than the surrounding jungle so people could use them as landmarks. The Maya also used some pyramids as tombs for important government officials.

Some Maya pyramids are as tall as a 20-story building.

WHY WAS ONE MAYA BALL GAME DEADLY SERIOUS?

In many countries, baseball is the ball game of choice for thousands of fans and players. In Maya society, the ball game wasn't as much fun—at least not for the losers. It gave new meaning to the baseball phrase *"you're outta here!"* The Maya used a rubber ball to play the game on a stone court. The goal of the game was to pass the ball and get it through a ring without having to touch the ball with your hands. The winners were treated as heroes and given a great feast. The losers were put to death.

WHY DID THE MAYA CIVILIZATION DISAPPEAR?

For 1,200 years, Maya society dominated life in Mexico and Central America. Maya cities were crammed with people. Then the Maya civilization disappeared. NASA scientists say drought and **deforestation** may have caused the Maya civilization to collapse. The Maya destroyed their land to make a living in hard times. They cut down the jungle to grow corn to feed their ever-growing population. They also cut trees for firewood and for building homes.

Why did the Trojan War start?

The Trojan War is one of the greatest events in Greek **mythology**, and is the focus of such epic Greek poems as the *Iliad* and the *Odyssey* of Homer. According to legend, the war began following the kidnapping of Helen of Sparta by Paris, the prince of Troy. Sparta was a **city-state** in ancient Greece. Helen's husband, Menelaus (Men-uh-LAY-us), was the king of Sparta. He went to war with Troy to get his wife back.

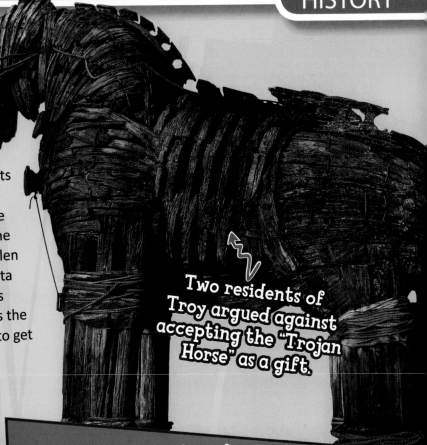

Two residents of Troy argued against accepting the "Trojan Horse" as a gift.

HOW DID ZEUS BECOME KING OF THE GREEK GODS?

In Greek mythology, Zeus is the king of gods and the ruler of Mount Olympus, home of the gods. Zeus is also the god of sky and thunder. Zeus became the supreme god by overthrowing his father. He then drew straws with his brothers Poseidon and Hades, to see who would rule the world. Zeus won.

Why didn't the people of Troy fear the Trojan horse?

During the Trojan War, which is part of Greek mythology (in other words it may not have happened), Troy, a city located in modern-day Turkey, was pitted against the ancient Greeks. According to the myth, after a 10-year **siege** of Troy, the Greeks built a huge wooden horse. Several Greek warriors crept into the belly of the horse and hid. As the Greeks pretended to leave, the Trojans pulled the horse into their walled city, believing it was a victory trophy. No such luck. The hidden warriors crept out of the horse at night, opened the front gates, and let the rest of the Greek army in. They destroyed Troy and won the war.

Where did the Vikings go in North America?

The Vikings arrived in America long before Columbus.

The Vikings of Scandinavia set foot in the New World 500 years before Columbus arrived. It was Leif Erikson who was one of the first Europeans to land in America. Around the year 1002, he set sail from Greenland and reached what is today Baffin Island in Canada, west of Greenland. He then sailed on to Labrador and into the Gulf of St. Lawrence. He built a settlement at L'Anse aux Meadows, Newfoundland, which served as a base camp for future Viking exploration of North America. The Vikings traded with the native population. Eventually the natives became unfriendly, and the Vikings returned to Greenland, but continued to sail to Canada for timber.

WHY DID SOME CONSIDER THE VIKINGS BARBARIANS?

Although some Vikings of Scandinavia had no problems raiding towns and villages along the coasts of Britain and France ("Viking" is Scandinavian for "pirate"), most Vikings were peaceful traders, artisans, craftspeople, and merchants. The Vikings developed a complex farming society and a wide-ranging trade network in Eastern Europe that brought goods from as far away as the Orient. Vikings got their reputation as barbarians because Viking men would often join groups on voyages of plunder, attacking seaside towns and taking what they wanted.

Did Vikings really have horns on their helmets?

Although football's Minnesota Vikings have painted horns on their helmets, the real Vikings of Scandinavia did not wear horned helmets. Although many ancient cultures wore horned helmets for ceremonies, the helmets fell out of fashion by the time of the Vikings. If you see a painting of Vikings with horns on their helmets, you know the artist made a mistake.

Why did the Crusades begin?

Led by kings and knights, Christian warriors marched into the Middle East in an attempt to capture the "Holy Land" near Jerusalem from Muslim rulers. Those invasions were known as the Crusades. The First Crusade began in 1095. A highly-trained force, including 4,000 knights on horseback and 25,000 foot soldiers, moved east in 1096. There were a total of eight crusades. The last one started in 1270.

WHY WERE KNIGHTS IMPORTANT IN MEDIEVAL EUROPE?

During the Middle Ages (5th to 16th centuries) in Europe, it was everyone's duty to obey the king. Landowners were the most powerful people. Kings gave their friends, known as noblemen, land for their loyalty. In turn, the noblemen relied on armed warriors, known as knights, to help them in battle and protect their land.

WHY DID PEOPLE BUILD CASTLES?

During the first part of the Middle Ages, people generally built homes out of straw, mud, and stone. Some even built small churches, but not much else. By 1000 A.D., people in Europe started erecting impressive churches. The Europeans also built castles out of giant stones for protection from attacking armies. Many medieval castles had towers and **spires**, steeply-pitched roofs, and magnificent archways. Building a castle was often long and difficult.

Invading armies built new weapons to attack fortified castles.

Why is the printing press one of the **most important inventions of all time?**

You probably think your iPod, iPhone, or your laptop are the most important inventions in the history of the world. Think again! Most people say the invention of the printing press was way more important. Prior to the mid-1400s, there was only one way to print a book—by hand. It was a long, hard, and expensive process. Only a few books existed, and only rich people could afford them. That all changed when Johannes Gutenberg, a German inventor, invented the printing press in 1440. The press made it easier to print books, and more people learned to read.

Before he was a printer, Johannes Gutenberg was a goldsmith.

WHAT WAS THE FIRST BOOK GUTENBERG PRINTED?

The first book to roll off the Gutenberg printing press was the Bible. No one knows how many Gutenberg printed, but some guess he produced at least 180 volumes. Some of Gutenberg's Bibles still exist today.

How did the printing press help change world history?

The printing press made it possible for individuals to read the ideas of other people. It also provided a way to share news and information. Some religious and political leaders feared such information and ideas would threaten their hold on power. They were right. The ideas of philosophers, priests, politicians, and others gained a wide audience around the world because of the printing press. In many cases, those ideas started revolutions, as some people tried to change the way they lived and the way their governments worked.

Was the 100 Years War really 100 years long?

From 1337 until 1453, the French and British fought what historians call the Hundred Years War. Although the historians were off by 16 years, the war started in May 1337, when France's King Philip VI tried to capture British territory in southwestern France. Of course, the British did not like this. Over the next 116 years, both sides fought, with brief periods of uneasy peace. The war ended when the French forced the British from the European continent.

Longbows were highly accurate weapons.

Medieval knights faded away at the end of the Hundred Years War.

WHAT IS A LONGBOW?

The longbow played an important role throughout the Hundred Years War. It was used mainly by the English and it was more accurate than the crossbows the French used. Some historians say a trained archer using a longbow could shoot 12 arrows a minute. Others say skilled archers could fire 24 arrows in 60 seconds. The arrows from a longbow could kill a soldier at 100 yards (91.4 m) and wound a soldier who was standing 250 yards (228.60 m) away.

WHY WAS THE HUNDRED YEARS WAR A TURNING POINT?

The war marked the last time the English would try to control territory on the continent of Europe.

105

WHY DID EUROPEAN EXPLORERS CAUSE PROBLEMS IN THE NEW WORLD?

Columbus opened the door for Europeans to come westward. Once the Europeans saw the New World, they began looking for gold and other treasures. They did not find gold, but the Europeans began exploiting the natives. They made slaves of the native people and took their land. The Europeans also brought weeds, rats, and diseases, which killed millions of natives.

Why did Christopher Columbus sail to America?

If Christopher Columbus had a GPS system, he might not have reached the Americas. Instead, he would have made it to Asia. When Columbus sailed across the Atlantic in 1492, no one in Europe knew a New World existed. Columbus was looking for a short route to Asia. At the time, ships traveled around the tip of Africa to get to the Orient. When Columbus arrived in the Americas, he first believed he was in Asia.

WHY WAS CHRISTOPHER COLUMBUS ARRESTED?

Christopher Columbus first landed in Hispaniola, where he left some of his crew to set up a colony. When he returned in 1493, he found the colony in confusion. He tried to restore order. Many colonists went back to Spain and complained about how he ran the colony. A royal governor then came to America and arrested Columbus. When Columbus returned to Spain, the king and queen spared him from going to prison.

What was the Industrial Revolution?

The Industrial Revolution changed how products were made (in factories instead of at home). The Industrial Revolution began in England in the mid-1700s mainly because England had a wealthy economy that made it possible for businessmen to build factories. England was also home to brilliant scientists, which led to great inventions that helped factories make products.

Machines helped launch the Industrial Revolution.

Today's factories are much bigger than those of the Industrial Revolution.

WHY WERE MACHINES IMPORTANT TO THE INDUSTRIAL REVOLUTION?

Machines were the engines that drove the Industrial Revolution. Machines allowed factories to make goods faster and cheaper. The steam engine, for example, replaced the water wheel as a source of power. New devices, such as the carding machine, which turned wool into yarn, replaced old-style tools such as the spinning wheel and handloom.

Were George Washington's teeth really made from wood?

There are many myths surrounding George Washington's teeth. While it's true that Washington had several sets of false teeth, none were made of wood. His dentures were fashioned from gold, hippopotamus ivory, lead, and human and animal teeth. Washington's dentures had springs that helped them to open and bolts to hold them together.

George Washington had several pairs of false teeth.

DID GEORGE WASHINGTON REALLY CHOP DOWN A CHERRY TREE?

Like the wooden teeth myth, there seems to be no truth to the story that George Washington chopped down a cherry tree or that he confessed to his father, "I cannot tell a lie." The story was made up by man named Mason Weems shortly after Washington's death. Weems made up the story to show how honest the "Father of Our Country" was.

WHY DID GEORGE WASHINGTON OWN SLAVES?

George Washington was a slave-holding farmer from Virginia. Washington inherited 10 slaves from his father. Eventually, he owned more than 300 slaves who lived at Mount Vernon, his home in Virginia. Washington's slaves worked the fields and his property, but when he died, they were freed.

Washington's slaves toiled at his home in Mount Vernon, Virginia.

Why did the American Revolution begin in Massachusetts?

For more than a decade, tensions between Great Britain and the American colonies ran high. The British had passed a series of laws to increase their control over the colonies. Colonists protested these laws, particularly in Massachusetts. To punish the colony, the British refused to let Massachusetts rule itself. Instead, the king sent royal governors to run the colony. In 1775, Britain declared Massachusetts (particularly Boston) to be in rebellion. The British sent troops to put down the "revolt."

WHERE WAS PAUL REVERE GOING ON HIS MIDNIGHT RIDE?

On the night of April 18, 1775, Paul Revere made one of the most famous trips in American history. An American patriot named Dr. Joseph Warren asked Revere to ride to Lexington to warn John Hancock and Samuel Adams that the British were about to arrest them. After Revere crossed the Charles River by boat, he waited for a signal to see which route the British were taking. Two lanterns hanging in the bell-tower of Christ Church meant that the British would row across the Charles River. One lantern meant they would march out of Boston. When two lanterns appeared, Revere borrowed a horse and hurried off. He was not alone that night. William Dawes and Dr. Samuel Prescott took a different route. Both warned the countryside that the British were on the move.

WHY DID AMERICAN COLONISTS WANT TO BREAK FREE FROM BRITISH RULE?

In 1763, the French and Indian War had come to an end. The cost of the war was huge. Britain forced the American colonies to pay for it. Tensions between the British king and the Americans grew as taxes and government rules were forced on them. By 1775, American colonists were growing more unhappy with British rulings toward the colonies. Eventually, the two sides clashed in battle, and the American Revolution began.

What is **Charles Darwin's** theory of evolution?

When Charles Darwin published his book *The Origin of Species* in 1859, it sent shockwaves around the world. In the book, Darwin outlined his theories of natural selection and **evolution**. According to Darwin, plants and animals, including humans, changed over time. He said that organisms inherit new characteristics that allow them to survive and reproduce, a process known as natural selection. Darwin said that all living things came from a single common ancestor.

Charles Darwin first wanted to be a clergyman.

Why did Charles Darwin sail the world?

In 1831, Darwin set sail on the *HMS Beagle* as an unpaid **botanist**. The ship was on a British scientific expedition. In South America, Darwin found fossils of animals that were extinct, but resembled modern species. In the Galapagos Islands in the Pacific Ocean, Darwin found many plants and animals of the same species that had different characteristics. These and other observations led Darwin to his theories about how life evolved over millions of years.

The HMS Beagle

WHY DID DARWIN WAIT YEARS BEFORE PUBLISHING *THE ORIGIN OF SPECIES?*

Upon his return to London, Darwin secretly worked on his theory. He said evolutionary change required millions of years. It took years before he published *The Origin of Species*. Darwin waited to make public his findings because he knew the book would create a controversy. Many scientists, who were also members of the Church of England, were critical of Darwin's theories because he challenged the Biblical version of Creation. Most scientists agree that Darwin's theories about how life on Earth evolved continue to hold up today.

Slaves used the Underground Railroad in all kinds of weather.

What was the Underground Railroad?

The Underground Railroad wasn't a real railroad. It was a system that allowed escaping slaves from the South to travel to the North to be free, especially during the 1850s and '60s. The slaves followed routes called "lines." People who helped the slaves along the lines were called "conductors." Houses along the way where slaves hid were "stations." The slaves themselves were called "packages."

Why did escaping slaves go to Canada?

The number of slaves escaping to freedom angered many Southerners. After the U.S. Congress passed the Fugitive Slave Act in 1850, it became illegal to keep escaped slaves in Northern states. So, escaping slaves had to travel to Canada, a foreign country, to be free.

WHY WAS HARRIET TUBMAN AN IMPORTANT CONDUCTOR ON THE UNDERGROUND RAILROAD?

Harriet Tubman was a slave in Maryland when she escaped from her owner and fled North to freedom. Later, she helped many people escape slavery. For 10 years, Tubman traveled to the slave-holding South to lead escaping slaves north to freedom. She later became a leader in the movement to free all slaves.

Slaves were often bought and sold at public auctions.

Why did Americans buy and sell slaves?

Long before the United States was the United States, slaves from Africa toiled on southern plantations and in the homes and ports of northern cities. The first slaves came to America in 1619, when a Dutch ship brought 20 enslaved Africans to the Virginia colony of Jamestown. Slaves were a cheap source of labor. They worked on sugar, rice, and cotton plantations. They also worked in homes in the North. Slavery became important in keeping America's economy growing. Eventually, 4 million slaves were brought to America.

Why was the Civil War fought?

The issue of slavery was the chief reason the nation was split during the Civil War (1861–1865). Southern lawmakers wanted slavery to expand as America grew. The South feared President Abraham Lincoln would abolish slavery so it decided to **secede**, or leave, the Union. Lincoln had to keep the Union together. The Civil War began. By 1863, the war's focus changed from reuniting a divided nation to freeing the slaves.

Why did the Titanic sink?

The passenger ship *Titanic* was on its first voyage on April 14, 1912. The luxury liner hit an iceberg 380 miles (611.55 km) southeast of Newfoundland, Canada. The iceberg tore a huge hole into the side of the ship, which began filling with water. The ship broke in half and sank more than 2 miles (3.22 km) to the bottom of the North Atlantic.

Poor construction materials doomed the Titanic.

Why did the *Titanic* sink so fast?

Scientists say *Titanic* sank so quickly because tiny metal fasteners called rivets that held the ship together didn't work the way they were supposed to. Scientists examined a few of the ship's rivets, which they brought up from the depths of the Atlantic. They found the metal fasteners were of such poor quality that they easily broke. When *Titanic* hit the iceberg, the heads of the rivets broke off, popping the fasteners from their holes and opening up a huge hole in the ship. If *Titanic*'s builders had used better materials, the ship would have stayed afloat longer, allowing more time for rescue ships to arrive.

WHY DID SO MANY PEOPLE DIE WHEN THE *TITANIC* SANK?

The *Titanic's* engineers believed the ship was unsinkable, so they didn't provide enough lifeboats for all passengers and crew. The ship had only 20 lifeboats that could carry about half of the 2,200 people on board. Only 705 people survived the sinking.

What war was called the "War to End All Wars"?

When World War I (1914–1918) began, no one imagined how brutal it would become. Soldiers used new weapons, such as the tank, poison gas, and the machine gun, for the first time. When the war ended, more than 40 million people had died. The war was so bloody and so devastating that many believed it would be the last war humans would ever fight—"The War to End all Wars."

Why did the United States enter World War I?

By 1917, most Americans sided with the British and French, who were fighting the Germans in World War I. Americans were angry because German submarines, or U-boats, were sinking American ships suspected of aiding Britain and France. In 1915, the Germans sank a passenger liner, killing 128 Americans. The Germans stopped the U-boat attacks for a while, but began the attacks again in 1917. On April 6, 1917, the U.S. Congress declared war on Germany.

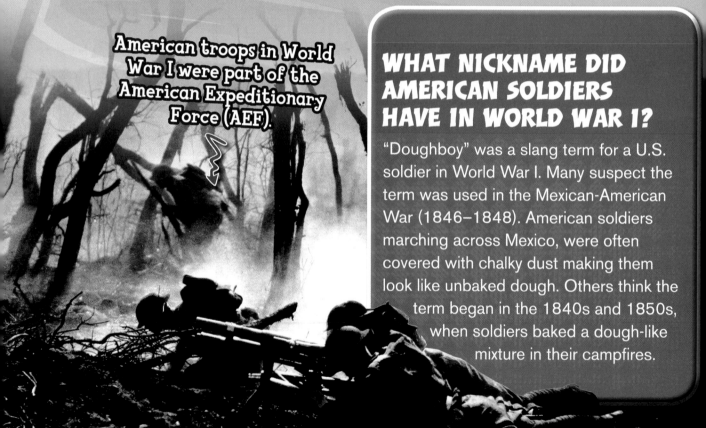

American troops in World War I were part of the American Expeditionary Force (AEF).

WHAT NICKNAME DID AMERICAN SOLDIERS HAVE IN WORLD WAR 1?

"Doughboy" was a slang term for a U.S. soldier in World War I. Many suspect the term was used in the Mexican-American War (1846–1848). American soldiers marching across Mexico, were often covered with chalky dust making them look like unbaked dough. Others think the term began in the 1840s and 1850s, when soldiers baked a dough-like mixture in their campfires.

What was the Cold War?

The Cold War wasn't a war fought with weapons. It was a war of ideas and competition between two systems of government: democracies and communism. The two nations most involved in the Cold War were the Soviet Union (Russia) and the U.S. When World War II ended, the U.S. wanted to stop communists from taking over other countries. The two nations made military treaties with other nations. Each side tried to gain superiority in space, sports, and weapons. The Cold War ended with the fall of the Soviet Union in 1991.

For years, only the Soviet Union and the United States had nuclear missiles.

What was the Iron Curtain?

In 1946, Winston Churchill, who led Great Britain during World War II, coined the term "Iron Curtain" to describe communist influence in Eastern Europe. In a speech to American students at Westminster College in Missouri, Churchill said an "iron curtain" had descended across Europe. On one side of that curtain, Churchill said, communist governments ruled with an iron fist. Throughout the Cold War, Churchill's Iron Curtain symbolized the differences between communism and the western democracies. It also symbolized the physical boundary that divided Europe at the time.

WHAT WAS THE BERLIN WALL?

The Berlin Wall divided West Berlin and East Berlin during much of the Cold War. After World War II, Berlin and Germany were divided. The Soviet Union and its allies controlled East Germany and East Berlin. The United States and its allies controlled West Germany and West Berlin. On August 13, 1961, the East German government built a wall to stop those living in East Berlin from escaping to the West. On November 9, 1989, the Berlin Wall came down when communism began to lose its influence in Eastern Europe.

What was the Great Depression?

The 1930s were a terrible time in the United States. On October 27, 1929, the stock market crashed, sparking the Great Depression, the biggest economic disaster in U.S. history. Banks closed, factories went out of business, and people closed their stores. Farmers could not pay their mortgages, and people lost their homes. People lost their jobs and had little money to spend on the things they needed. When Franklin Roosevelt became President in 1933, about one out of every eight Americans was out of work.

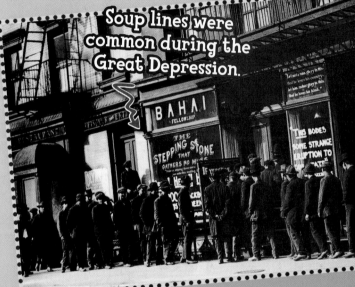

Soup lines were common during the Great Depression.

WHY DID FRANKLIN ROOSEVELT USE A WHEELCHAIR?

When Franklin Roosevelt was 39 years old, he became ill with polio. The disease left him unable to walk. Although he spent the rest of his life in a wheelchair, he did not let the disease ruin his life. He became governor of New York, and later, President of the United States.

1882 1982
USA 20c
Franklin D. Roosevelt

When did the Great Depression end?

The Great Depression lasted about 10 years. When Franklin Roosevelt became President, he started programs to increase jobs and slow the economic problems the Depression had created. Roosevelt pushed through Congress his "New Deal" legislation. America became a welfare state—a state that looks after the economic and social well-being of its citizens. The New Deal created 42 new government agencies designed to create jobs, control banks, and provide money to people out of work. These actions, plus the beginning of World War II, which enabled millions to find work in factories, slowly brought an end to the Great Depression.

Why did the Japanese bomb Pearl Harbor?

By the end of 1941, Japan had expanded its influence in South Asia. It had invaded French Indochina earlier in the year. In response, the United States cut off oil supplies to Japan. As Japanese and U.S. officials tried to work out a peaceful solution, the Japanese military came up with a secret plan to destroy the U.S. Navy fleet based in Pearl Harbor, Hawaii. The attack occurred on December 7, 1941. The next day, the United States declared war on Japan.

More than 2,000 people died at Pearl Harbor.

WHY DID THE U.S. DROP ATOMIC BOMBS ON JAPAN?

World War II ended in Europe in April 1945. The U.S. and its allies could then focus on winning the war against Japan. President Harry Truman ordered two atomic bombs to be dropped on the island nation, hoping this would force the Japanese to surrender. The first bomb exploded over Hiroshima on August 6, 1945. Three days later, another bomb exploded on Nagasaki. The Japanese surrendered on August 15.

WHY DO KIDS SEND PAPER CRANES TO JAPAN?

Each year, kids from around the world send paper cranes as a sign of peace to the Children's Monument in Hiroshima's Peace Park. The cranes were inspired by the story of Sadako Sasaki, who was two when the bomb was dropped on Hiroshima. The radiation made her sick and she died of leukemia in 1955. While in the hospital, she began folding cranes believing that if she folded 1,000 she would be granted one wish. She only folded 644 before her death but her friends folded the other 356 for her.

Why were some military codes in World War II spoken in Navajo?

The Japanese were experts at breaking secret U.S. military codes used for sending messages. A Marine named Philip Johnston, who knew how to speak Navajo, had an idea to use the Navajo language to send messages. Only a few people outside the Navajo nation knew the language. The Navajos who sent and translated messages were called code talkers.

HOW DID NAVAJOS COMMUNICATE WITH EACH OTHER DURING THE WAR?

To send a coded message, the Navajos strung together words in their own language. Code talkers receiving the message changed each Navajo word into English. They used only the first letter of the English word to spell out the code when they received the message.

WHY COULDN'T THE JAPANESE BREAK THE NAVAJO CODE?

The Japanese weren't even aware the Navajo language existed. Although the Japanese could hear the messages, they could not crack the code. To keep the Japanese guessing, the code talkers used three Navajo terms for most English letters. For example, "moasi" (Cat), "tia-gin" (Coal), and "bas-goshi" (Cow), all stood for the letter C.

Japanese internment camps in the U.S. were located mostly in the West and Southwest.

WHY DID THE U.S. FORCE JAPANESE AMERICANS TO MOVE TO PRISON-LIKE CAMPS DURING WORLD WAR II?

After the Japanese bombed Pearl Harbor, there was fear on the West Coast that Japanese Americans would act as spies. Following the attack, President Franklin Roosevelt signed an order allowing the U.S. military to move people of Japanese ancestry to internment camps where they were guarded at all times. About 120,000 Japanese, 70,000 of whom were U.S. citizens, were sent against their will to these prisons.

WHEN DID THE U.S. APOLOGIZE FOR THE JAPANESE CAMPS?

In 1988, Congress passed, and President Ronald Reagan signed, a law apologizing for the camps. He said the decision to lock up the Japanese Americans was based on "race, prejudice, war hysteria, and the failure of political leadership." It was the end to a sad chapter in U.S. history.

Were any Japanese Americans arrested for spying during World War II?

No. In fact, the government created an all-Japanese American military unit to fight in Europe. The unit received many awards and medals.

Nathan Hale was one of George Washington's spies.

WHO SAID "I REGRET THAT I HAVE BUT ONE LIFE TO LOSE FOR MY COUNTRY"?

Nathan Hale, one of America's most famous spies, uttered that phrase just before the British executed him during the American Revolution. George Washington had asked him to spy on the British in New York City. Writings have described Hale as a spy who couldn't keep quiet. Hale made friends with a man who Hale didn't know was a British spy. He invited Hale to dinner where Hale talked about his mission. British soldiers arrested Hale, and hanged him the next morning.

What does "Four score and seven years ago" mean?

"Four score and seven years ago" was the beginning of Abraham Lincoln's *Gettysburg Address*. It was a way to say the year "1776," which was when the Declaration of Independence was signed. A "score" equals 20 years. "Four score" equals 80 years. Add seven more years, and the total is 87. Lincoln was in Gettysburg, Pennsylvania, in November 1863 (87 years after the colonies declared their independence), when he gave the *Gettysburg Address*.

The *Gettysburg Address* was only 267 words long.

Why do languages spread from **place to place?**

People speak English not only in the United States, but in England, India, and other countries. Portuguese is not just spoken in Portugal, but also in Brazil. French is spoken in France and in Quebec, Canada. There are about 6,800 languages around the globe. Languages have a shared system of sounds, words, and sentences that people can use to communicate thoughts, ideas, and emotions. There are many reasons why languages spread from country-to-country. The chief reason is that as people move, they carry their language with them.

الجوازات
Immigration

صالة تسليم الحقائب
Baggage Claim

English is one of the world's most common languages.

WHY IS ENGLISH THE OFFICIAL LANGUAGE IN SO MANY COUNTRIES?

English developed in... where else? England! English spread throughout the world because England controlled a great empire during the 18th, 19th, and early 20th centuries. People in nations that were once part of the British Empire continue to speak English. Today, there are about 350 million people who speak English as their first language.

Why are some languages disappearing?

Experts say that half of the world's languages will be dead by 2050. Some say that 90 percent of languages could be extinct by 2100. Languages die when they are not passed to the next generation. For example, school children in Alaska are learning only two out of 20 native Alaskan languages. The other 18 languages are in danger of disappearing.

Why are there holes in Swiss cheese?

Raise your hand if you think mice chew the holes in Swiss cheese! Mice have nothing to do with the production of the cheese, but bacteria do. Bacteria are single-celled organisms that multiply very fast. All cheese is made by adding bacteria to milk. The milk begins to curdle as bacteria eat. Three types of bacteria help make Swiss cheese. Two types of bacteria produce lactic acid. The third type of bacteria live off the lactic acid and give off bubbles of carbon dioxide. Those bubbles form the holes that give Swiss cheese its unique look.

The holes in Swiss cheese comes from bursting bubbles.

Why isn't all bacteria bad for you?

While some bacteria can make a person sick, other bacteria are good for you. Some bacteria help in food digestion. Other types of bacteria live on skin and in the mouth to protect people against the bad bacteria that can make them sick.

Good bacteria are prime ingredients in making cheese.

WHY DOES CHEESE NEED TO AGE TO TASTE GOOD?

Age doesn't make everything better, but it sure improves a wheel of cheddar cheese! Some cheese is tastier when it is eaten at a very young age. However, some cheese is extremely yummy if it is left on the shelf for weeks or months. Aging allows the enzymes and bacteria in the cheese to transform it into a tasty snack. Each type of cheese requires a different aging period.

Why do leaves change color?

Red, orange, yellow, and brown—these are the colors of autumn. Trees make their own food through a process called **photosynthesis**. During photosynthesis, trees use the sun's light to turn water from the ground and carbon dioxide from the air into oxygen and **glucose**, a kind of sugar. Trees use glucose as food for energy. During the winter, there is not enough sunlight for photosynthesis. So, trees shut down their tiny food-making factories. When that happens, **chlorophyll** (needed for photosynthesis and to give leaves their green color) fades, leaving the leaves bright orange, red, and yellow.

When leaves fall, trees stop making food.

Why do leaves fall?

It is late autumn and all the leaves have fallen. As sunlight decreases in autumn, the hollow tubes that carry sap into and out of a leaf begin to close. As that happens, a layer of cells forms at the base of the leaf stem. Those cells help the leaf separate from the branch, and it falls to the ground.

WHY IS GRASS GREEN?

Grass is green because it is filled with chlorophyll. Chlorophyll is the green pigment that absorbs sunlight during photosynthesis.

Why is
water wet?

Take a bath—get wet! Go for a swim—get wet! Get smacked in the noggin with a water balloon—get wet! Believe it or not, water isn't wet. Wetness is just a feeling we experience. In fact, liquids, such as water, aren't wet. Liquids have special qualities that make us feel "wet" when we touch them. When we change those qualities, water can be as hard as rock—think ice, or as light as air—think steam.

Why is water
tasteless?

Like wetness, taste is a perception or experience brought to you by your taste buds. Taste buds allow people to taste things that are salty, sour, bitter, or sweet. Humans experience taste because molecules in food and drink interact with taste receptors in the mouth. Candy is sweet because the molecules in sugar react with our taste receptors. Water contains nothing to trigger our taste receptors. So, water seems to be tasteless to us. Drink up!

WHY IS WATER IMPORTANT FOR LIFE?

All life as we know it depends on water. Why is that? All the reactions that take place in our bodies to carry on life need a fluid to work. All living things use water to carry nutrients and other important chemicals to organs and cells. Water also helps our bodies flush out waste.

Without water, life as we know it would not exist.

Why do chemical reactions occur?

A chemical reaction occurs when two or more substances interact. Water forms when two hydrogen atoms react with one oxygen atom. An automobile rusts because iron atoms in the steel react with oxygen atoms in the air.

Hydrogen
H_2

Oxygen
O

Water
H_2O

A chemical reaction causes water to form.

Why does mixing vinegar and baking soda cause an "explosion"?

How many times have you made a tabletop volcano? What do you use to give the volcano its pop? You use baking soda and vinegar, of course! When you mix vinegar and baking soda, a chemical reaction takes place. The acetic acid in vinegar—stuff that gives vinegar its sour taste—reacts with the sodium bicarbonate (a **compound** in baking soda) to form something entirely different—carbonic acid. Carbonic acid breaks down into carbon dioxide and water. The escaping carbon dioxide gas creates the bubbles you see as they overflow like a gushing volcano.

HOW IS A GAS DIFFERENT FROM A SOLID OR LIQUID?

Matter, which is anything that has mass and takes up space, comes in three states: solid, gas, and liquid. An ice cube is a solid. Solids have tightly packed particles. Helium is a gas. In a gas, particles move fast and don't stay close together. Water is a liquid. Liquid particles move around, but don't have a shape.

Why does a bee make honey?

Bees buzz near blooming flowers to find sweet nectar. A single honeybee will visit between 50 and 100 flowers on one trip. Bees take the nectar and turn it into honey. Bees store honey in hives to eat later when flowers are not blooming.

Why do bees dance?

Bees dance to communicate with each other. Scout bees, for example, look for flower beds bursting with pollen. If they find one, they fly to the hive and "dance" to tell the other bees what they found. Some bees also dance the "round dance" to tell other bees that pollen is near the hive.

Thousands of bees can live in one hive.

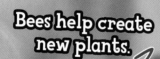

Bees help create new plants.

WHY DO BEES POLLINATE FLOWERS?

As bees look for food, they help create new plants through **pollination**. Bees take pollen from the male parts of a flower and move it to the female parts of a flower. The flower then creates a seed. From that seed a new plant grows. In the United States, bees pollinate 95 different crops.

Why does a pencil look like it's **bending in water?**

If you hold a pencil straight up in a glass of water and look through the side of the glass, it looks as though the pencil is bending. Light is playing tricks on your eyes. When light beams enter water, the water slows down the beams of light. This causes the light to bend away from its original path, a process called **refraction**.

Light can play tricks on your eyes.

WHY DO SOME PEOPLE SNEEZE IF THEY LOOK INTO THE SUN?

Have you ever come from a dark room into the bright sunshine and started to sneeze? You might suffer from photic sneeze reflex, which causes people to sneeze in the sudden appearance of bright light, especially sunlight. No one knows exactly why the reflex exists. Some scientists think the cause is located in a person's nervous system.

Why does it look like there's **water** on a road when it is **sunny outside?**

Drive down the road on a hot summer day, and you might see a puddle of water in the middle of the street even though it has not rained. The puddle is a mirage, or vision caused by bending light. A light beam can change direction, or bend, when it passes from cooler air to hotter air. On a hot sunny day, the road's pavement is warmer than the air above it. When light hits the boundary between the cooler and warmer air, it bends just enough to make a "puddle" seem to appear on the roadway.

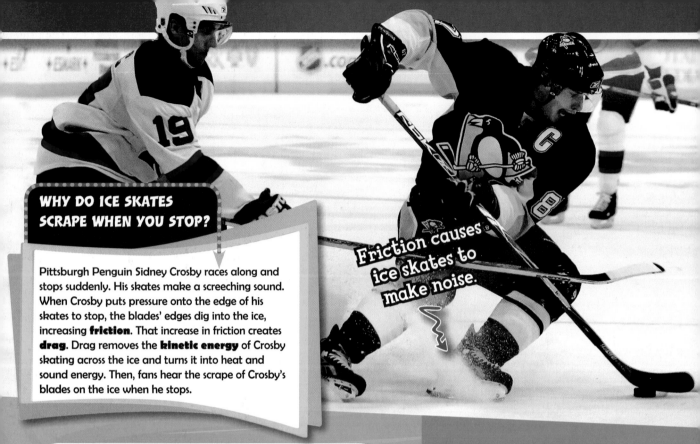

WHY DO ICE SKATES SCRAPE WHEN YOU STOP?

Pittsburgh Penguin Sidney Crosby races along and stops suddenly. His skates make a screeching sound. When Crosby puts pressure onto the edge of his skates to stop, the blades' edges dig into the ice, increasing **friction**. That increase in friction creates **drag**. Drag removes the **kinetic energy** of Crosby skating across the ice and turns it into heat and sound energy. Then, fans hear the scrape of Crosby's blades on the ice when he stops.

Friction causes ice skates to make noise.

WHY DOES SALT MELT ICE?

When the temperature is below 32°F (0°C), water freezes into ice. Since salt water doesn't freeze until a slightly lower temperature, adding salt to an icy sidewalk or road can melt ice, as long as the temperature isn't lower than the freezing point of salt water.

Why can we skate on ice?

Although the question seems simple enough, scientists are still searching for an answer. They used to believe that ice under a skate is slippery because the pressure of the skate's blade lowers the melting temperature of the ice surface. As the ice melts, the blade glides across the thin layer of water. That water refreezes as soon as the blade passes. Some scientists now believe that water molecules on the surface of ice vibrate faster because nothing is holding them down. As a result, the molecules remain unfrozen, making ice slippery.

Why does baking soda get rid of odors in the fridge?

Because no one wants to smell last night's fish dinner, people often put a box of baking soda in the fridge to soak up the smell. Odors, such as those from sour milk, are created by acids in the food. Molecules of these acids rise up in the air causing the odor. Baking soda absorbs these acid molecules and neutralizes them, removing the odor. However, over time the powder becomes less effective, especially when it mixes with water vapor. A crust forms on top of the powder, limiting the baking soda's ability to soak up the smell.

WHY DON'T SWEATY HANDS SMELL AS BAD AS SWEATY FEET?

Feet smell because they sweat. In fact, there are more than 250,000 sweat glands on feet. Bacteria feed off the salt and water of sweat. The bacteria then give off waste, which causes a nose-numbing odor on shoes and socks. Although hands have the same amount of sweat glands as feet do, they are not usually wrapped in socks and shoes. Sweat evaporates on hands before bacteria can feed, whereas sweat on feet does not evaporate as quickly.

Why does my breath smell?

Brushing your teeth can help stop bad breath.

Bad breath, also known as halitosis (hal-uh-TOH-sis), is caused by odor-producing bacteria that grow in your mouth. If you don't brush or floss regularly, the bacteria can surround bits of food left in your mouth and between your teeth. When that happens, bacteria release smelly sulfur compounds, which make your breath stink.

Why does eating a hot pepper
burn my tongue?

If you have ever bitten into a jalapeño or a chili pepper, you probably felt pain because it was so hot. Hot peppers are steamy because they contain capsaicin (cap-SAY-sin). Capsaicin is a pepper plant's natural defense against animals that might want to eat it. Birds, however, aren't affected by capsaicin. That's a good thing, because birds help spread the plant's seeds so more pepper plants can grow.

WHY DO PEOPLE LIKE SOME FOODS AND DISLIKE OTHERS?

Scientists say genetics play a role in why we like some foods and not others. Researchers say our genes decide the number of taste buds we have on our tongues. A Yale University researcher says that people with more taste buds can experience the taste, texture, and temperature of food better than those with fewer taste buds. As such, the more taste buds a person has, the more foods that person will probably enjoy.

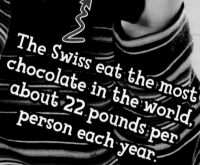

The Swiss eat the most chocolate in the world, about 22 pounds per person each year.

Why can eating chocolate candy make people hyper?

Chocolate candy and many soft drinks contain sugar and caffeine. It's the caffeine, not the sugar, that can make a person jumpy or hyper. Some parents blame sugar for their children's **hyperactivity**. But most researchers now say that sugar does not make most children "bounce off the wall." Some studies show that artificial, or human-made, food dyes are responsible for increased hyperactivity in kids.

Why do helium balloons float?

Up, up, and away! If you have ever let go of a helium-filled balloon at a fair or a birthday party, you know that the balloon floats away. Why? Helium is a gas that is lighter than the surrounding air. The balloon rises because the helium displaces, or pushes away, the air around the balloon. This is known as **buoyancy**. Balloons are a danger to wildlife, especially sea creatures, so don't let balloons float away!

Why does a spoon get hot in a pot of boiling water?

A process called **conduction** is the reason that heat energy travels from a pot of boiling water to a spoon sitting in the pot. During conduction, the molecules in the hot water are moving quickly. They pass heat to other molecules around them. In time, they pass heat to the spoon sitting in the pot.

The helium in balloons is lighter than the air.

HOW DO ICE CUBES MAKE DRINKS COLDER?

As ice absorbs the heat from a drink, the ice gets warmer and begins to melt and turns into water. The cooler water from the ice makes the drink colder. The more ice you put in a drink, the quicker the ice absorbs the heat.

How do clouds form?

Clouds form when the sun warms air containing water vapor. As warm air rises, it becomes colder. Gradually the water vapor in the air turns into tiny drops of water. The molecules in the water grab hold of tiny bits of dust, pollen, and other types of pollution. Clouds form as the water molecules condense onto these particles.

How does snow form?

Snow begins its life as an ice crystal. Ice crystals form when the temperature in a cloud is below freezing, 32°F (0°C). If the temperature of the air just below the cloud is also below freezing, the crystals cling together and fall to the ground as snowflakes.

HOW LARGE CAN SOME SNOWFLAKES BE?

As snow hits the ground, the average snowflake is about 0.5 inches (1.3 cm) across. If the falling ice crystals stick together, some flakes can measure more than 4 inches (10 cm) across and be made up of as many as 100 separate ice crystals.

Why does laundry **detergent** remove dirt from clothes?

Laundry detergents are made up of chains of carbon and hydrogen molecules. While some of those molecules love water, some of them hate water. When you put detergent in the washing machine with dirty clothes, the water-hating soap molecules bind to the dirt. When you turn the washing machine on, it swirls the water. This allows the soapy water around the dirt to pull the grime away from the clothes.

Why does dish soap clean greasy plates?

Dish soap molecules are made up of long chains. One end of the chain attaches itself to the grease on the dinner plate, prying the scum loose. The grease is then carried off by rinsing with water.

Detergent contains water-hating molecules.

WHY DOES OIL FLOAT ON WATER?

Try this experiment: Pour a few drops of vegetable oil into a glass of water. The oil floats on top of the water, spreads out, and makes a light covering. Why? First, most oils weigh less than water. Second, most oils do not dissolve in water, but tend to stick together. When oil goes into water, oil molecules cluster near each other at the surface.

Although oil floats on water, oil spills can be difficult to clean up.

What is that big red spot we see when we look at **Jupiter** through a telescope?

Jupiter's Great Red Spot is an ancient storm resembling a hurricane on Earth. No one knows why the storm is red. All they know is that the storm has been raging for more than 300 years—that's how long humans have been observing Jupiter through a telescope. Jupiter's red spot is big enough to hold three Earths. Scientists say that Jupiter's red spot, however, is shrinking.

Jupiter's red spot will one day disappear.

Why is a year on Jupiter much longer **than a year on Earth?**

Did you know if you're 13 years old on Jupiter, you would be about 156 years old on Earth? A year on Jupiter is equal to almost 12 years on Earth. In other words, it takes Jupiter 12 Earth years to go once around the sun. The days on Jupiter are much shorter than the days on Earth, however. It takes Jupiter just 9.8 hours to turn on its axis, while it takes Earth 24 hours.

You can see Jupiter's bands through a small telescope.

WHY ARE THERE BANDS AROUND JUPITER?

The colorful bands around Jupiter are evidence of complex weather systems. The light-colored bands are named "zones," while the dark-colored bands are called "belts." High-speed winds blow the belts and zones in opposite directions, causing multi-colored patterns to form. The colors come from the tiny chemical and temperature differences between the neighboring bands.

Why does temperature change?

Temperature is a degree of hotness or coldness that we measure using a thermometer. Temperature is related to how fast the molecules of a substance are moving. The faster the molecules move, the higher the temperature. So molecules in boiling water move much faster than those in ice water. Molecules slow down as the hot water cools, bringing the temperature from hotter to cooler.

WHY IS IT HOTTER AT THE EQUATOR THAN AT THE NORTH AND SOUTH POLES?

The sun's rays warm the Earth. Although there is the same amount of solar radiation hitting the Earth at the poles and at the equator, the sun's rays fall more directly on the equator than on the poles. That is because of Earth's curvature, or rounded shape. This is why temperatures at the equator are much warmer than temperatures in the Arctic or Antarctica.

This lion lives in Kenya, a nation in Africa that straddles the equator.

WHY IS IT COOLER ON TOP OF A MOUNTAIN THAN AT ITS BASE?

Air is made of billions of tiny air molecules. Gravity holds those molecules close to Earth's surface. The sun's rays first heat Earth's surface. That heat then radiates up, warming the surrounding air molecules. Air molecules are less able to store heat energy the higher they go. So, it is much cooler at the top of a mountain than near its base.

It's frosty at the top of a mountain.

Why does glue have
sticky properties?

Glue has two properties that make it sticky: adhesion and cohesion. Adhesion is the glue's ability to hold objects together. Cohesion is the glue's ability to hold onto itself. These two properties help glue stick to surfaces by seeping into the cracks and holes of an object's surface and then hardening and locking onto that surface.

WHY IS TAPE STICKY?

Tape is a band of flexible material treated on one or both sides with temporary glue that can stick to surfaces.

Glue has two properties that make it sticky.

Rubber bands stretch because of chains of stringy molecules.

WHY ARE RUBBER BANDS ABLE TO STRETCH, TWIST, AND CHANGE BACK INTO THEIR SHAPES?

That concept is known as elasticity. Rubber contains carbon and hydrogen. Rubber bands get their stretch because the molecules of these elements bond together into long flexible chains called polymers. Pulling a rubber band causes the polymers to untwist and straighten. When you release the rubber band, the polymers return to their original form.

How did e-mail start?

You've got mail! People send billions of e-mails by using the Internet. The first person to send an e-mail, or electronic mail, was Ray Tomlinson. In 1971, Tomlinson was working on a computer system that would later become the Internet. He found he needed a better way to leave messages on the computers of his fellow workers. He used the @ sign to separate names of users from names of their computers on the **network**. So, today we address e-mails like this: janedoe@earthlink.net.

E-mails can travel around the globe in seconds.

Why do some e-mails bounce back?

Sometimes you send a person an e-mail, and it "bounces" back to you. When your e-mail system makes contact with someone's e-mail server, the server decides if it will let the message through. If it doesn't, the server "bounces" the message back. Why? Perhaps the address is wrong, or misspelled. There may not be enough room on the system, or an e-mail system may fail.

WHAT DOES *HTTP* MEAN?

The Internet is a very complex system that connects millions of computers to one another. In 1989, a British scientist named Tim Berners-Lee invented hypertext transfer protocol, or http, a series of linked words that allows users to navigate the Internet. In short, Berners-Lee invented the first Web browser.

137

WHY DO I HAVE TO TURN OFF MY CELL PHONE IN AN AIRPLANE?

"Please turn off all electronic devices including cell phones and computers." If you have ever flown in an airplane, you are familiar with those words. Flight attendants always make sure passengers in flight do not use their cell phones.

What's the reason for this? Airplanes contain many radios that do a lot of different things. One type of radio allows pilots to talk to ground control. Another type of radio lets air traffic controllers know where the plane is located. Cell phone transmissions could interfere with how these radios work, especially if the cell phones are on the same radio frequency as the plane's equipment. If that happens, it is possible that those signals could create equipment problems within the plane.

WHY ARE CELL PHONES LIKE TINY RADIOS?

Cell phones send and receive radio signals. Their networks are divided into "cells." Cells are specific areas that have a special station to receive and send radio signals. Each station has an **antenna**, more commonly known as a cell phone tower. The antenna transmits signals just like a radio station. When you turn on your cell phone, it searches for a signal from the nearest cell phone tower. If you're too far away from a tower, or if the signal is too faint, you will lose the signal…and the call.

What do 2G and 3G on a cell phone stand for?

Cell phone networks are broken down into digital networks. The name 2G network is short for second generation network. That means 2G networks are more advanced than the previous network. The name 3G network is short for third generation network. 3G networks can carry more information than 2G networks. You can make a simple phone call on a 2G network or send a text message, but you can't send music clips or videos. You can send large amounts of data on 3G networks very quickly. Products such as smartphones use 3G networks.

How are HDTVs and standard TVs different?

HDTV stands for high-definition television. HDTVs work by picking up and decoding digital signals. When a TV station broadcasts in high definition, the TV station changes pictures and sounds into trillions of bits of electronic data. An HDTV takes that digital data and changes it back into pictures and sounds. A standard TV turns radio signals into sounds and pictures. Radio signals do not carry as much information as digital signals.

WHY DO DIGITAL MOVIE PROJECTORS HAVE SHARPER PICTURES THAN STANDARD PROJECTORS?

Digital Light Processing, or DLP, will soon be coming to a theater near you. Instead of using film, DLP projectors use pictures and sounds that have been digitized, or converted, into trillions of bits of information. Digital projectors bounce light off millions of tiny mirrors onto a movie screen, producing a crystal clear picture with high-quality sound.

HDTVs are becoming more popular and are quickly replacing standard TVs.

Why is HDTV **clearer and sharper** than standard TV?

HDTVs have more lines of information and pixels (tiny colored dots) per picture than standard TVs, resulting in a clearer picture that is much sharper than a standard, non-HD, television.

139

WHY DO ALL RADIO STATIONS HAVE "CALL LETTERS"?

When the radio was first invented, it was used as a wireless telegraph. Messages between ships at sea were transmitted in Morse Code—a series of electric "dots" and "dashes." Early radio operators identified themselves with short call letters that they could easily tap out in Morse Code. At the time, people made up their own call letters. Soon things got very confusing. To avoid this confusion, the world's nations got together and gave each radio operator a set of call letters to use. That's why today every radio station (and every TV station, too) has its own unique set of call letters.

There are about 44,000 radio stations in the world.

Why do U.S. TV and radio station names start with W or K?

You can find WABC in New York, and KCAL in Los Angeles. Each name represents the call letters the stations use. Early in the 20th century, the U.S. government split the nation into east and west, using the Mississippi River as a dividing line. The government ruled that the names of all new radio stations (and later, TV stations) west of the Mississippi River would begin with a "K," while the names of all stations east of the river would begin with a "W." The number of radio and TV stations was growing rapidly, and using different letters for east and west increased the number of available sets of call letters.

WHAT DID GUGLIELMO MARCONI DO?

Guglielmo Marconi was the first to figure out how to transmit electrical signals from one place to another over invisible, naturally occurring radio waves. Radio waves travel through the air at the speed of light— 186,000 miles (299,000 km) per second.

How are party balloons made?

The balloons you see at birthday parties are made out of liquid rubber called latex. Latex balloons are shaped from a mold. A mold is a shaped container. Workers first coat the mold with substances such as alcohol or a type of salt which make the latex stick to the mold. Next, workers dip the mold into a pot of hot latex. The molds are then put in a 200°F (93.33°C) oven for 20 minutes. When the latex is hard, machines strip the balloons from the molds and put them in packages.

The first Macy's parade was held in 1924 to celebrate Christmas!

HOW HIGH DO HELIUM BALLOONS FROM THE MACY'S THANKSGIVING PARADE GO?

Those special balloons can be up to four stories tall. Some of the character balloons can float 10 stories above the crowd!

How do microwave ovens cook food?

You're late for school. Pop a toaster cake in the microwave, push some buttons, and within seconds you can have a fast and easy breakfast. Microwave ovens can heat food in seconds and cook meals in minutes. Inside the microwave is a special tube called a magnetron that changes electricity into high frequency microwaves. Microwaves are a form of electromagnetic energy. Microwaves cause water and food molecules to vibrate very quickly. This creates friction that produces heat, which can cook or warm up food fast.

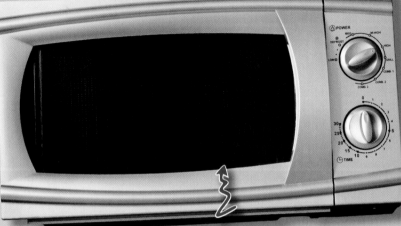

The first microwave oven went on sale in 1967.

WHY DO PEOPLE MICROWAVE SPONGES?

Heating a sponge in a microwave for two minutes can kill the bacteria that can settle on the sponge.

WHY CAN'T I USE A METAL CONTAINER IN A MICROWAVE?

Microwaves can heat the metal to the point where it can cause a fire or produce harmful gases.

Microwaves can kill bacteria on a sponge.

Why does an
airplane fly?

"Success... Four flights...Longest 57 seconds...Inform press. Home for Christmas." Orville Wright sent this message to his father in December 1903. He and his brother, Wilbur, had become the first humans to fly in a gasoline-powered aircraft. The Wright brothers realized that as the propeller pulls the plane forward, air moves across the top of the wing faster than it moves below the wing. That causes less air pressure on top of the wing than below. This creates lift, which causes the plane to soar.

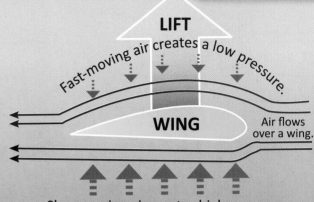

LIFT

Fast-moving air creates a low pressure.

WING

Air flows over a wing.

Slow-moving air creates high pressure that pushes upward, causing the lift necessary for flight.

Orville Wright was the first person to fly in a gasoline-powered airplane.

How does a
jet airplane fly?

Jet engines combine air under immense pressure with fuel. When a spark ignites the mixture, it creates a jet of hot gases that escapes, producing forward movement called thrust. Once the jet is moving forward, the same principles that create lift in propeller-driven airplanes take over.

WHAT DO ROTORS ON A HELICOPTER DO?

On a helicopter, lift, or upward movement in the air, is produced by a copter's propellers called rotors. If a helicopter had only the large main rotor on top of the craft, it would spin in circles. A small rotor near the tail keeps the helicopter from whirling out of control. While airplanes can only fly horizontally, helicopters can move vertically and even hover in mid-air.

Eyepiece Lenses

Prism

Objective Lens

Light

Why do binoculars let me see faraway objects?

Binoculars are like a mini-telescope that people can hold in their hands. Inside binoculars are lenses that take in light from an object. The lenses magnify the image. The light passing through the front lens and **prisms** then travels down the tubes and through lenses in the eyepieces, magnifying the image even further.

WHY CAN I SEE MY REFLECTION IN A MIRROR?

Most mirrors are made from glass and thin layers of aluminum or silver. You can see your reflection because light energy hits the smooth surface of a mirror and reflects back to you like a rubber ball bouncing off a wall. If the mirror is bumpy, light will bounce all over the place, and you won't be able to see your reflection as clearly.

WHY CAN I SEE THINGS THROUGH MICROSCOPES THAT ARE TOO SMALL TO SEE WITH JUST MY EYES?

Microscopes are super-powerful magnifying glasses that can make itsy-bitsy things easy to see. In an optical microscope, a light shines upward reflecting off the object being viewed. The reflected light passes through a special lens. That lens brings the object into focus inside the microscope's tube. The image is then magnified by a second lens in the eyepiece.

The first microscope was built in 1590 by Hans and Zacharias Janssen.

How does a light bulb shine?

Every time you turn on a standard run-of-the-mill light, something amazing happens. When you flick the switch, you are allowing electricity to flow. Inside a light bulb is a thin coil of metal wire called a filament. The electricity flows through the filament, heating the wire to a temperature of more than 4,500°F (2,482°C). At such a high temperature, the filament glows, producing light. The glass bulb protects the filament, and keeps oxygen away from the wire. If air was inside the bulb, the wire would burn very quickly. The glass also keeps gases, such as argon and nitrogen, inside the bulb, which allows the filament to last a long time.

HOW DOES A CANDLE BURN?

People have been lighting candles for centuries to find their way in the dark. When a person lights a candle with a match, the wick begins to burn. The flame slowly travels down the wick until it hits the wax. The flame's heat then begins to melt the wax surrounding the base of the wick. The liquid wax is drawn up to the tip of the wick inside the flame, providing fuel for the fire. The cycle repeats itself until all the wax is gone.

WHY ARE FIREWORKS COLORFUL?

"Ooh! Ahh! Ooh!" There's nothing like a fireworks display on the Fourth of July. Fireworks are colorful because they are packed with different chemicals. When these chemicals are lit, they burst into different colors. One type of chemical gives off a reddish color, while others produce green, white, and blue colors.

How did the first instant camera work?

Long before digital cameras, an inventor named Edwin Land created the first camera in 1947 that took instant pictures. It was called the Polaroid. Polaroid cameras worked just like ordinary film cameras, with one huge difference: the film developed itself. The film in a Polaroid camera contained layers of chemicals. Some of the chemicals were sensitive to blue, green, and red light. When a person snapped a picture with a Polaroid camera, the camera captured the image on a layer of silver. As the camera spit out the film between two rollers, chemicals inside the film reacted with one another, allowing an image to appear on the layer of silver.

Polaroid cameras developed the film almost immediately.

WHY DO CAMERAS NEED A FLASH WHEN TAKING PICTURES IN THE DARK?

A camera needs light to capture an image. When it's dim or dark, a light flashing for a brief second throws enough light over the area so the camera can snap the photo.

Why do people in photographs sometimes have red eyes?

If a subject is close to a camera lens, the burst of light from the camera's flash goes through to the back of the subject's eyeball. The **retina** inside the eye is rich in red blood vessels. When the light strikes those red blood vessels, it reflects the red color seen in the picture.

You need light to snap a photo.

Why did **Alexander Graham Bell** invent the telephone?

"Mr. Watson, come here! I want to see you." Those nine words made Alexander Graham Bell famous. They were the first words spoken on the telephone. Bell didn't set out to invent the telephone. He was looking for a way to invent a better telegraph machine. On March 10, 1876, Bell and his assistant, Thomas A. Watson, were working on what would become the first telephone. "I … shouted into [the mouthpiece] …'Mr. Watson—Come here—I want to see you.' To my delight he came and declared that he had heard and understood what I said." Bell later told his father that he could see the day when "friends converse with each other without leaving home."

In 1915, Bell places the first coast-to-coast telephone call.

HOW DOES A TELEGRAPH WORK?

Long before iPhones and smartphones, people communicated over long distances using the telegraph. Invented by Samuel Morse, the telegraph let people communicate with electronic dots and dashes sent over a wire. To spell out the words, a telegraph operator had to tap a transmitting key at one end of the line. That key turned the electricity "on" (dots) and "off" (dashes). At the other end of the wire, a person listened to the dots and dashes and translated the coded message.

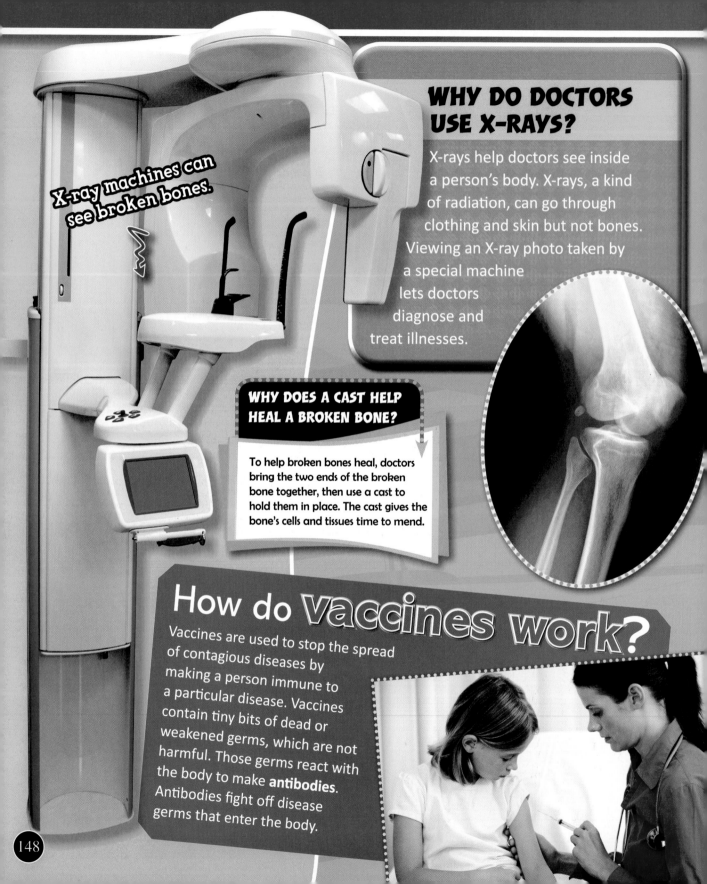

X-ray machines can see broken bones.

WHY DO DOCTORS USE X-RAYS?

X-rays help doctors see inside a person's body. X-rays, a kind of radiation, can go through clothing and skin but not bones. Viewing an X-ray photo taken by a special machine lets doctors diagnose and treat illnesses.

WHY DOES A CAST HELP HEAL A BROKEN BONE?

To help broken bones heal, doctors bring the two ends of the broken bone together, then use a cast to hold them in place. The cast gives the bone's cells and tissues time to mend.

How do vaccines work?

Vaccines are used to stop the spread of contagious diseases by making a person immune to a particular disease. Vaccines contain tiny bits of dead or weakened germs, which are not harmful. Those germs react with the body to make **antibodies**. Antibodies fight off disease germs that enter the body.

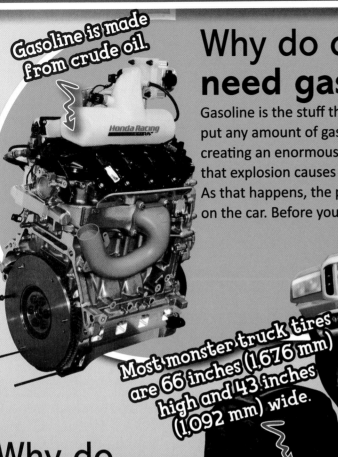

Gasoline is made from crude oil.

Why do cars and trucks need gasoline?

Gasoline is the stuff that powers most car and truck engines. When you put any amount of gasoline in a small place and light it, the fuel explodes, creating an enormous amount of energy. In a car engine, the force of that explosion causes the engine's **pistons** to move up and down. As that happens, the pistons turn a crankshaft that turns the tires on the car. Before you know it, you're traveling down the road.

Most monster truck tires are 66 inches (1,676 mm) high and 43 inches (1,092 mm) wide.

Why do some cars get **better gas mileage** than others?

Some cars can go farther on a gallon of gas than others. Why? Among other things, the engines of good gas mileage cars burn gasoline more efficiently than other cars. Also, cars get good gas mileage by moving at a steady speed, having properly inflated tires, and by having an engine that is in good working order.

WHY ARE TIRES MADE OF SEVERAL MATERIALS AND NOT JUST RUBBER?

Car tires are made from a combination of rubber, fabrics, and thin steel cables. The cables and fabric give the tire the strength and firmness it needs. Steel belts are especially important to make sure the tire doesn't puncture easily. The steel also helps the bottom of the tire stay flat on the road's surface so it moves smoothly. The grooved rubber on the tire's outside is called the tread.

Pencils contain graphite.

Why is there no lead in a lead pencil?

"Lead pencils" got their name when someone in 16th century England found shiny bits of stone near the roots of a fallen tree. People started to call the flashy substance "blacklead." They soon found the mineral was good for writing. Blacklead was really graphite, a form of carbon. The first pencils, then, were sticks of natural graphite wrapped in string or a wooden tube. The term "blacklead pencil" was first used in 1565. Today, some pencils are made of charcoal and other materials.

WHY DOES AN ERASER ERASE?

How many times have you worn down your pencil eraser to the nub in math class? An eraser, which is a chunk of rubber, is able to remove your mistakes by picking up tiny pieces of graphite particles left on a piece of paper by a pencil. An eraser does its job because the molecules in the rubber are stickier than the molecules on the paper. So the graphite from the pencil sticks to the eraser. Of course, erasing is a messy job. You have to wipe away the bits of eraser that come off as you erase.

Molecules in an eraser are stickier than paper molecules.

What are **crayons** made of?

Crayons are made of pigments and paraffin wax—the same type of wax used on fruits and vegetables to make them shiny in the grocery store. The two are mixed together and poured into molds, which are then allowed to cool.

Crayons are colored wax.

WHY CAN YOU ERASE SOME INK FROM A SHEET OF PAPER?

Often you can't erase a mistake if you are writing with a pen—unless you use a pen with erasable ink. These pens use ink made out of rubber cement. The rubber makes it easier to wipe away a mistake. However, within 10 hours, the ink will dry and harden on the paper so you won't be able to erase any more.

How are colored pencils made?

Colored pencils are a combination of several ingredients: extenders (the body of the "lead"), binders, which hold the ingredients together, and pigments, which give the pencils their color. The ingredients are mixed together with hot water to form a paste. The paste is then rolled into sheets and pressed into long cylinders. A machine forces the paste through a small tube and cuts it into thin layers. Once the paste dries, it is sandwiched between two pieces of wood and cut into individual pencils.

Why do people call Broadway the "Great White Way"?

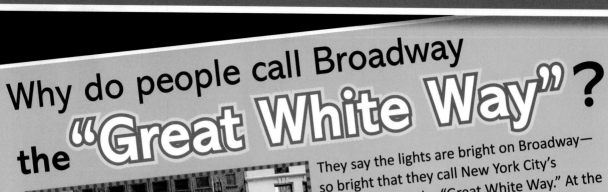

They say the lights are bright on Broadway— so bright that they call New York City's theater district the "Great White Way." At the beginning of the 20th century, 16 theaters were on Broadway itself and many others were located near the famous avenue. The fronts of all these theaters blazed with lights to call attention to the plays.

HOW DID THE TRADITION OF THE NEW YEAR'S BALL DROP IN TIMES SQUARE START?

In the early 1900s, the *New York Times* tower was the tallest building in Manhattan and the focus of a large New Year's Eve celebration. The all-day festival ended with fireworks set off near the base of the tower. In 1907, the city outlawed the fireworks display. Founders of the celebration decided to have a 700-pound (318 kg) iron and wood ball with 100 25-watt bulbs lowered on the building's flagpole at midnight to signal the end of 1907 and the beginning of 1908. The tradition continues today.

Times Square in New York City is known as the "Crossroads of the World."

What was the first rock 'n' roll song?

No one person invented rock 'n' roll. That's why it's not easy to figure out what was the first rock 'n' roll song. Although you may not know some of these first rock musicians, many fans believe that Bill Haley's *Rock Around the Clock* (1954) was the first rock 'n' roll record. Many others believe it was Elvis Presley's *That's All Right Mama* (1954). Others say a song called *Rocket 88* (1951) by Jackie Brenston was the granddaddy of them all.

What was the first sound recording?

Thomas Edison was the inventor of the phonograph. In 1877, Edison tested his new invention by recording the nursery rhyme "Mary Had A Little Lamb" on a cylinder of metal.

Thomas Edison, inventor

WHAT WAS THE FIRST MUSIC VIDEO PLAYED ON TV?

Although it might be hard to believe today, once upon a time music videos didn't exist. That all changed on August 1, 1981, when the new music network MTV televised the first music video— *Video Killed the Radio Star*. Sung by the British rock band The Buggles, the song described a singer whose career was cut short by television.

What was Mickey Mouse's original name?

Mortimer Mouse? That was Mickey's first name!

In 1928, Walt Disney created a cartoon mouse he called Mortimer Mouse. Disney's wife didn't like the name Mortimer, so she renamed the character Mickey. Mickey Mouse made his movie debut in a cartoon called *Steamboat Willie* that same year.

WHY DID SNOOPY AND CHARLIE BROWN FLY TO THE MOON?

Good grief! Snoopy and Charlie Brown are two of the most beloved cartoon characters. Created by Charles Schulz, the boy and his beagle actually did once fly to the moon. In June 1969, NASA sent a space capsule named *Charlie Brown* and a landing craft named *Snoopy* to the moon aboard *Apollo 10*. Astronauts piloted *Charlie Brown* to within 8 miles (12.87 km) of the lunar surface. Neither craft landed, however.

Where did the famous "Hollywood" sign come from?

Overlooking Hollywood, California, on the top of Mount Lee, is a sign with one word: "Hollywood." In 1923, the sign spelled out "Hollywoodland" to advertise new homes in a neighborhood called "Hollywoodland." Over the years, the sign began to fall apart. When the Hollywood Chamber of Commerce decided to repair the sign, it took the last four letters off, and today it reads "Hollywood."

Why are movies sometimes called "flicks"?

In the early 1900s, filmmakers would film a movie using a camera powered by a hand crank. Depending on the strength of the cameraman's arm, the speed of the film was between 8 and 22 frames, or moving pictures, per second. To make the images look like one continuous picture, filmmakers put a small slate between each frame of the film. This resulted in a constant flickering on the movie screen, and the term "flicks" was born.

WHEN WAS THE FIRST "TALKING" MOVIE?

Imagine watching a movie with no sound. To understand what the actors were saying you had to read words that came onto the screen. Music came from a person in the theater playing the piano. That's what the first movies were like. It all changed in 1927, when the first movie with sound, known as a "talkie," was made. The movie was called *The Jazz Singer*, with an actor named Al Jolson.

Why is this painting of a **soup can** so famous?

Andy Warhol must have liked soup—Campbell's soup to be exact. Warhol was one of the most important artists of the 20th century. In his early years, Warhol was trying to find a way to become as popular as some of the other artists of the day. An art gallery owner suggested that Warhol paint a can of Campbell's soup. He did. Instead of using an actual can of soup as his guide, however, Warhol painted a huge soup can using images from a magazine. Once it hung in an art gallery, the painting thrilled many people because it was so different. Warhol took a common product and turned it into art.

What is surrealist art?

Surrealist art often shows objects that have no business being together or near one another. The most famous surrealist artist, Salvador Dali, painted melting watches and weird landscapes.

WHO WAS GRANDMA MOSES?

The artist known as Grandma Moses was born Anna Mary Robertson in 1860. In 1887, she married Thomas S. Moses. Although she had painted for most of her life, Grandma Moses didn't become famous until she was almost 80 years old, when a well-known art collector saw a few of her paintings. Three of those paintings were put on display at the Museum of Modern Art in New York City, making Grandma Moses a well-known artist.

Salvador Dali's "The Dream"

Who was **Pablo Picasso?**

Pablo Picasso was an artist. Unlike most artists, he wasn't interested in showing how people and objects actually looked. Instead, he imagined what would happen if those objects were squished against the canvas. As a result, his paintings had a lot of circles, squares, and other shapes. This type of painting is known as cubism.

Why is *Mona Lisa* smiling?

Although the *Mona Lisa* doesn't have any eyebrows, her smile is what makes her portrait by Leonardo da Vinci, an Italian painter, so famous. Why she's smiling is anyone's guess. Experts believe the portrait, painted in the early 1500s, is of a 24-year-old woman. The shadows at the corners of her eyes and mouth leave people wondering what she is thinking.

WHAT DOES THE WORD IMPRESSIONISM MEAN IN ART?

Impressionism is a style of art where the artist captures just an *impression* of an object, person, or landscape rather than painting it in great detail. Claude Monet is one of the best-known impressionists.

Mona Lisa lived in Florence, Italy.

Who is the "real" Dr. Seuss?

You've probably read some books written by Dr. Seuss. Dr. Seuss's characters have unusual names, like Horton, the Cat in the Hat, Sam I Am, and the Grinch. But what about the author's name? Dr. Seuss isn't the real name of the writer of all those books. It is Theodore Seuss Geisel. He was not a real doctor. He added Dr. to his name because his father wanted Theodore to earn a doctorate degree as a college professor. More than 200 million Dr. Seuss books have been sold. They've been translated into 15 languages. In addition, his works have been made into television specials, movies, and a Broadway play.

Mike Myers played the character of the Cat in the Hat in the movie.

WHAT WAS DR. SEUSS'S FIRST BOOK?

And to Think That I Saw It on Mulberry Street was Dr. Seuss's first book. Almost 30 publishers turned it down. Luckily, a friend took the book to a friend whose company finally printed it. The story follows a boy who watches people and cars as they go by on Mulberry Street. The boy tries to think of a fanciful story to tell his father about what he saw, but finally tells him what really happened.

WHAT WAS SO SPECIAL ABOUT DR. SEUSS'S BOOK *THE CAT IN THE HAT* ?

Although he had written many other books, it was *The Cat in the Hat* that made Dr. Seuss famous. In the 1950s, many people started thinking that children's books were boring and didn't get kids to read. In 1957, Seuss wrote *The Cat in the Hat* to help children learn to read. The story is about a brother and sister alone in the house on a rainy day—until a cat in a silly hat enters their lives, turning everything upside down. The book became one of the most popular children's books of all time. Have you read it? Chances are you have!

Why did J.K. Rowling make Harry Potter an orphan?

Harry Potter is probably the most famous boy wizard of all time. He is also an orphan who misses his parents. When J.K. Rowling wrote the first Harry Potter book, *Harry Potter and the Sorcerer's Stone*, she had a personal reason to make Harry an orphan. In an interview with a British newspaper, Rowling said her mother died at the age of 45 without knowing Rowling was writing the first Harry Potter book. The loss of her mother led Rowling to make Harry an orphan.

WHY DID J.K. ROWLING MAKE QUIDDITCH AN IMPORTANT PART OF LIFE AT HOGWARTS?

Quidditch, a game played on broomsticks, is the most popular sport at Hogwarts—the school for wizards. J.K. Rowling has said she wanted to make sports an important part of the Harry Potter books because school sports are important in the lives of many kids. Although she wasn't very good at athletics herself, Rowling said she gave those who play Quidditch an important talent that she would have loved to have—the ability to fly.

HARRY POTTER and the Philosopher's Stone

J.K. ROWLING

HOGWARTS EXPRESS

Triple Smarties Gold Award Winner

WHERE DID J.K. ROWLING GET THE NAME "POTTER"?

A brother and sister who were children in Rowling's neighborhood were named Potter. Rowling has said that she liked their name better than hers because other kids made fun of her name.

Author J.K. Rowling

Why do some believe
William Shakespeare
didn't write all his plays?

For centuries, people have debated whether William Shakespeare wrote all of the plays and poems that bear his name. Many people have wondered: How did Shakespeare's humble origins produce such a genius? Some think that only a wealthy and highly educated person could write such great works. Some believe that others might have written many of the works thought to be by Shakespeare. But there is no proof that others wrote Shakespeare's plays and poems.

William Shakespeare was also an actor!

HOW MANY PLAYS DID SHAKESPEARE WRITE?

Begining in 1589, **William Shakespeare** wrote a total of 37 plays. Shakespeare never published any of his plays, however. They were printed after his death by two actors who wanted to show how much they liked him.

WHY DID MEN PLAY THE ROLES OF WOMEN IN SHAKESPEARE'S PLAYS?

Was Juliet played by a man in the first productions of *Romeo and Juliet*, back in the 1500s? The answer is yes. In the days of Shakespeare, some 500 years ago, plays were performed only by men. Women were not allowed on stage. That changed in 1660, when a female actress in England named Margaret Hughes played the leading female role in Shakespeare's play, *Othello*.

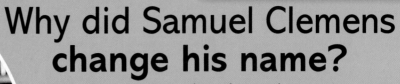

Why did Samuel Clemens change his name?

Does the name Samuel Langhorne Clemens ring a bell? Samuel Clemens was Mark Twain, one of the greatest American writers of all time. Born on November 30, 1835, Samuel Clemens changed his name to Mark Twain when he began writing for the *Territorial Enterprise*, a Virginia City, Nevada, newspaper. Before he became a writer, Clemens was a steamboat pilot on the Mississippi River. On a riverboat, the term "mark twain" was used to tell the pilot how deep the water was.

WHY DID MARK TWAIN VOLUNTEER AS A CONFEDERATE SOLDIER DURING THE U.S. CIVIL WAR?

Like many others in the South, Mark Twain wanted to become a soldier during the Civil War (1861-1865). However, Twain wasn't a very good soldier. His unit broke up after only two weeks when they found out Union soldiers were nearby. Clemens later wrote, "I knew more about retreating than the man that invented retreating."

WHY DID MARK TWAIN WRITE *THE ADVENTURES OF HUCKLEBERRY FINN?*

When he was a child growing up in Missouri, Mark Twain believed that Southern slaves were property. As he got older, however, his views changed. He realized that slavery was wrong. In *The Adventures of Huckleberry Finn*, Twain writes of the injustices of slavery. The book's main character, Huck, helps a runaway slave named Jim. Jim has escaped from Miss Watson after learning she might sell him to another slave owner. Jim does not want to go. Huck breaks the law to help Jim.

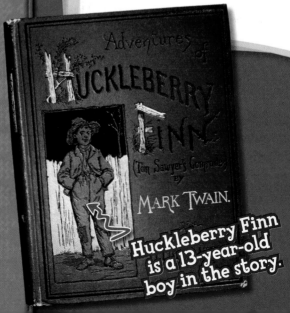

Huckleberry Finn is a 13-year-old boy in the story.

161

Why are baseball fields different sizes?

Not all baseball fields are the same size. While the rules of Major League Baseball spell out the exact size of the infield, the outfield is a different story. Each ballpark has different dimensions. According to the rules, the distance from home plate to the nearest fence in fair territory must be 250 feet (76.2 m) or more. Some teams use their field's measurements to their advantage. The Yankees often put strong left-handed hitters in the lineup to hit more home runs over Yankee Stadium's short right-field fence. The Red Sox fill their lineup with right-handed hitters to clear the short left-field fence at Fenway Park.

Only infields in baseball parks have the same dimensions.

WHY WERE FOOTBALL FIELDS' SIZES CHANGED FROM 110 YARDS TO 100 YARDS?

The dimensions of an American football field are the same: 100 yards (91.44 m) from one goal line to another. American football fields used to be 110 yards (100.58 m) long. The size of the field gradually changed over the years because some of the rules changed.

WHY WAS THE ZAMBONI MACHINE INVENTED?

In the early 1940s, Frank Zamboni had a cool idea for ice skating rinks. He wanted to make a machine that made ice smooth in minutes. Skaters' blades made grooves and bumps of shaved ice on the rink. Workers had to shovel away the shavings and spray water, which froze and filled the cracks, making the ice smooth. This took more than an hour. Frank Zamboni's machine did the job faster. Today, the Zamboni is seen on many ice rinks.

Who was the first woman on a Wheaties Box?

The makers of Wheaties like to say their cereal is the "Breakfast of Champions." But for many years, all the champions that appeared on a Wheaties box were men. That all changed in 1935, when Olympic track and field star Babe Didrikson became the first woman to appear on the box. At the time, the athletes—male or female—appeared only on the side of the box, not the cover. In 1984, Olympic gymnast Mary Lou Retton became the first woman to appear on the cover of the box.

Charlotte Cooper won a gold medal in tennis at the 1900 Olympic Games.

WHEN DID WOMEN START COMPETING IN THE OLYMPICS?

Women began taking part in the Olympic Games for the first time in 1900. The Games were held in Paris, France. There were 22 women who participated that year. A Mrs. Brohy and a Miss Ohnier of France were the first to compete. They played croquet.

Tara Lipinski was the youngest woman to win an Olympic gold medal in figure skating.

WHO WERE THE YOUNGEST WOMEN TO WIN OLYMPIC GOLD MEDALS?

At 13 years of age, Kim Yun-Mi of South Korea became the youngest Olympic gold-medal winner of all time. Kim was a member of the South Korean short-track speed skating relay team. That team won the women's 3,000-meter relay at the 1994 Winter Games. The youngest female to win an individual gold medal in the Winter Olympics was Tara Lipinski of the U.S. She won the gold in figure skating at the age of 15 in 1998.

Curling is like shuffleboard on ice.

What is the **sport** of curling?

Curling is one of the most popular sports in the world. It is similar to shuffleboard, except that curling is played on ice. Players slide a 42-pound (19 kg) stone disc toward a painted target on the ice to knock the opponent's stone out of the target area. Curling gets its name from the way the rock slides in a curl down the ice.

Why is fishing called **angling**?

When people go fishing, they use hooks. Hooks are known as angles because of their curved shapes. If you use a hook rather than a net to fish, you're an angler.

If you fish with a pole, you're an angler!

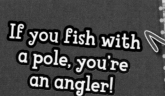

Why is a basketball **hoop** 10 feet off the ground?

Ten feet (3.05 m) is how high James Naismith put the hoops when he invented basketball. Naismith created the sport in 1891, by attaching peach baskets to two poles at the local YMCA in Springfield, Massachusetts. Each basket was 10 feet off the ground. The sport has kept the same basket height ever since.

Dr. James Naismith was born in Canada.

WHY DO SOME PEOPLE CALL BASKETBALL PLAYERS "CAGERS"?

In the early days of the sport, the first team to put their hands on an out-of-bounds pass that flew into the stands was given possession of the ball. When the ball went off the court, the players rushed for it, and fans often got hurt. To keep the ball in play at all times and to stop the accidents, someone decided to put a cage around the court. That's why basketball players are known as "cagers." The cages were removed in the 1920s when the out-of-bounds rule was changed. The new rule: when the ball goes out of bounds, play stops and the team that didn't touch the ball last is given posession.

HOW DID THE JUMP SHOT BECOME SO POPULAR IN BASKETBALL?

Before there was a jump shot, the set shot ruled. Players planted their feet on the court and shot the ball with one or both hands. Some players wanted to find a better way to score. As the game changed, players eventually developed the jump shot. In a jump shot, a player puts backspin on the ball. When the ball hits the rim or backboard, it changes velocity, and moves in the opposite direction of the spin. That results in more velocity toward the net, which helps the ball go into the basket.

Jump shots are the most important shots in basketball.

Why do football players put **black grease under their eyes?**

Football players put black grease under their eyes to make it easier to see the ball. The black grease is made mostly of wax and cuts down the sun's glare. Players began wearing the grease in the 1940s. They burned the end of a cork, let it cool, and used it to color their cheek bones black. Today, some players wear anti-glare stickers under their eyes.

WHY DO SOME FOOTBALL PLAYERS TAPE THEIR FINGERS?

College and pro football players often tape their fingers, believing the tape will make their grips stronger. However, a scientific study found that there was no difference in the grip strength of players whose fingers were taped and players whose fingers were not taped.

Why do football coaches wear headsets?

Football coaches wear headsets so they can talk to their assistant coaches who are sitting high above the field. Those coaches have a bird's-eye view of the game. They can see where mistakes are being made and can also tell which plays might work best. The coaches in the stands pass information to the coach on the field, who then passes it on to the team's quarterback or defense.

Why do race cars run on **bald tires**?

Tire treads—the pattern of deep grooves on the tires—make a car slower because of increased **friction** between the tire and the road. That's why race car tires are bald. In NASCAR races, smooth car tires allow for more speed. They have to be changed four to five times during a race.

WHAT PART DOES AERODYNAMICS PLAY IN RACE CAR DRIVING?

You can't talk about car racing without talking about **aerodynamics**, the study of how air flows over a surface. There are two major forces created by a car's movement. The first is drag. Drag is the resistance a car has when passing through air at high speeds. Drag takes away some of the car's power and speed. The second major force is called downforce. Downforce is air pressure pushing directly down on a car. Downforce helps the car grip the road.

WHY DO RACE CAR DRIVERS TAILGATE?

Race car drivers have perfected a racing technique called drafting. This is the aerodynamic effect that allows a tailgating car to move faster than the car in front. How does that happen? The lead car whizzes down the track, pushing the air in front out of the way. That opens a gap of air between the lead car and the second car. As the second car drives into the gap, not much air resistance pushes on its front end. So, the second car can move faster and save fuel.

Drafting allows race cars to go faster.

Why do some race cars have "wings"?

In car racing, the faster a car travels the greater its lift, or tendency to rise. When lift becomes too great, it causes the car to lose its grip on the road, making it hard to control. Race cars have wing-shaped parts called spoilers to fight off this lift. The spoilers create a downward force, which helps keep the car on the road.

spoiler

WHAT MAKES NASCAR CARS BETTER THAN THE "OLD" STOCK CARS?

Long ago, NASCAR drivers would "soup up" street cars and race them on a track. Today, NASCAR autos are wonders of science. Millions of dollars go into planning and designing them. Experts use computers to create the fastest NASCAR auto shapes and engines for the track.

WHY DO RACE CARS HAVE ROLL CAGES?

Race car drivers sit in metal roll cages made to protect them from crashes and rollovers. There are many different roll cage designs.

Old-time stock cars were not as fast as today's models.

HOW CAN SNOWBOARDERS DO SO MANY FANCY TRICKS?

Snowboarders can do many tricks because of friction. They shift, or move, their weight to have less contact with the snow on one side of the board, and to have more contact with the snow on the other side of the board. They also slide down the snow so fast that it gives them the power to jump and twist in the air.

Why do skiers wax their skis?

Wax on the bottom of a snow ski or snowboard allows it to slide down the slope with as little **friction** as possible. This means a skier can travel faster.

Science plays an important role in snowboarding.

Why do bobsledders push their sleds?

The faster a bobsled team pushes its bobsled at the start of their run, the more momentum the sled has. Momentum reduces the impact of air and friction on the moving sled, so it will go faster. Saving even one-tenth of a second during the start of a race can save one-third of a second on the entire bobsled run—the difference between winning and losing.

Did Abner Doubleday invent baseball?

People have been arguing for years about the origins of baseball. According to legend, Abner Doubleday invented the game in Cooperstown, New York, in 1839. Doubleday, however, never claimed he invented the game. A special panel in 1908, made up of baseball officials, gave Doubleday credit. If Doubleday didn't invent baseball, then who did? It's really anyone's guess.

Did Abner Doubleday invent baseball?

WHY DID THE BROOKLYN DODGERS HIRE JACKIE ROBINSON?

In 1947, when Branch Rickey, an executive with the Brooklyn Dodgers, hired Jackie Robinson, baseball's color line was broken. When Rickey became the Dodgers' general manager in 1942, he quietly began plans to bring black players to the team. Rickey picked Robinson because he was a good player, and he knew Robinson would be strong enough to handle the pressure of being the first African American in the big leagues.

WHY DID IT TAKE SO LONG FOR AFRICAN AMERICANS TO PLAY MAJOR LEAGUE BASEBALL?

African Americans couldn't play in the major leagues due to discrimination and racism. Many owners and players didn't believe blacks should play on white teams. Owners also thought whites wouldn't come to watch blacks play. So, African Americans formed a league of their own—the Negro League. White owners of major league ball clubs then rented their stadiums to Negro League teams when the major league teams were on the road. If the teams were **integrated**, there would be no more Negro League—and then no one would rent the stadiums. This meant white owners would lose money.

When was the **first forward pass** thrown in football?

For years, rules kept players from passing the ball. When President Theodore Roosevelt met with college officials to make the game safer, they changed the rules to allow passing. In 1906, Bradbury Robinson, quarterback for Saint Louis University, tossed the football to teammate Jack Schneider. The defense was so surprised by the pass that Schneider just walked into the end zone to score. Soon, other teams began throwing forward passes.

How did the **Green Bay Packers** get their name?

The Green Bay Packers were first owned by a local meat packing company called the Indian Packing Company. So, the team was named the Packers. The team was later owned by the Acme Packing Company. Although both companies went out of business, the name stayed.

WHY DO PLACE KICKERS SQUEEZE THE FOOTBALL?

Place kickers in football squeeze the football before they kick it to make it softer and rounder. They believe a new football does not travel as far as one that is softened up.

Where did the World Series get its name?

According to the *Baseball Almanac*, Major League Baseball had several championships during its early years. One, in 1884, was called "The Championship of the United States." Newspapers named the winning team "World Champions." The title stuck. In 1903, when Boston faced Pittsburgh in the championship series, people began calling it the "World Series."

The New York Yankees show off the World Series trophy they won in 2009.

HOW COME AMERICAN LEAGUE PITCHERS DON'T BAT?

When Major League Baseball adopted Rule 6.10 in 1973, teams were allowed to designate, or choose, a player to bat in place of the pitcher (generally the weakest hitter on the team). That chosen player was known as the designated hitter, or DH, for short. Today, the American League uses designated hitters, while the National League does not.

WHY IS BASEBALL'S NATIONAL LEAGUE CALLED THE SENIOR CIRCUIT?

There are two leagues in Major League Baseball—the National League and the American League. The National League was formed in 1876, and the American League began in 1901. Because the National League is older, people call it the Senior Circuit.

Ron Blomberg was baseball's first designated hitter.

Why does a curveball curve?

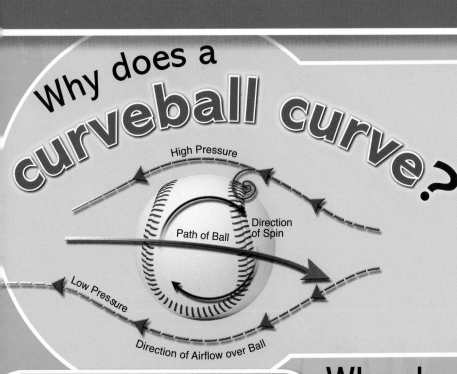

High Pressure

Path of Ball

Direction of Spin

Low Pressure

Direction of Airflow over Ball

A curveball moves to the right or left, and sometimes down. To throw a curve, a pitcher makes the ball spin sideways. As the spinning ball travels, low air pressure forms underneath it. The ball's stitching creates friction between the ball and the air. A high air pressure area forms on top of the ball, pushing the ball down to where the air pressure is the lowest. This imbalance causes the ball to curve toward one side.

WHY ARE ALUMINUM BATS MORE DANGEROUS THAN WOODEN BATS?

Many people say metal baseball bats are dangerous, especially for the pitcher on the opposing team. A ball flies off a metal bat faster than off a wooden bat. The faster the ball comes back to the pitcher, the less time the pitcher has to get out of the way, which can lead to injury.

Why do some youth baseball leagues use "soft" baseballs?

Many doctors advise young baseball players to use a soft type of baseball called a reduced injury factor (RIF) ball to protect their heads from serious injuries. The balls are the same size and weight as regular baseballs, but the inside of a RIF ball is made from a special foam. The foam can absorb more of an impact than a regular baseball if it should hit a player. This lessens the chances of getting hurt.

173

Why does a basketball bounce?

What happens when you try to dribble a basketball without any air in it? Nothing. Basketballs need pressurized air to bounce. Inside a basketball is a rubber pouch, or bladder. When that bladder is filled with air, it gives the ball a lot of **potential energy**. When the ball hits the ground, the air inside the ball compresses, or squeezes, as the skin of the ball flattens slightly at the bottom. Once the ball hits the floor and flattens, it bounces back. As the ball bounces, it returns to its original round shape.

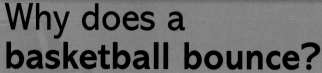

Inflated basketballs have a lot of stored energy.

Why is a basketball orange?

Paul "Tony" Hinkle was a college basketball coach who invented the orange basketball. Until the late 1950s, basketballs were dark brown. Hinkle said fans and players had a hard time seeing the ball. He worked with the Spalding Company to come up with an orange-colored ball that was easier to see.

WHY DOES A BASKETBALL RIM HAVE A NET?

There are two reasons why basketball rims have nets. The first reason is that nets slow down balls that are going through baskets. Without a net, a ball would fly off in many directions. The second reason is that nets make it easier for players and fans to see if a shot goes through the basket.

Why were the first Olympics held?

The first recorded Olympic Games were held in ancient Greece in 776 B.C., as a small festival to honor the god Zeus. The first Olympics had only a single event, a 210-yard (192 m) foot race called the *stadion*. The race took place in Olympia, in western Greece. The winner of that first race was a cook named Koroibos.

WHY DO OLYMPIC CHAMPIONS RECEIVE MEDALS?

The highest honor for any Olympic athlete is winning a gold medal. During the ancient Games, winners received olive wreaths to wear on their heads. The tradition of giving medals to the winners began at the Olympic Games in 1896. At that time, the winners who placed first did not get gold medals. Instead they received silver. Those who came in second took home a bronze medal, and third place finishers received nothing.

WHY ARE THE OLYMPIC GAMES SOMETIMES CALLED AN "OLYMPIAD"?

An Olympiad was a four-year period which the ancient Greeks used to keep track of time. After the first Olympics were held, the Greeks held the Games every four years. That's why people refer to the Games as an Olympiad.

Olympic gold medals are mostly made of silver, with a bit of gold.

Why are there dimples on golf balls?

Golfers found out very early that scuffed-up golf balls flew farther than smooth balls. That's why there are between 300 and 500 dimples on a golf ball. Dimples give a golf ball lift—or height—by creating a layer of fast moving air on the top of the ball and a layer of slower moving air on the bottom of the ball.

Good golfers like Michelle Wie use the slice to their advantage.

CAN SOME GOLF BALLS FLY FARTHER THAN OTHER GOLF BALLS WHEN HIT THE SAME WAY?

How a golf ball is made impacts how far it will fly. One-piece balls are solid, with no layers. They are poorly made golf balls. A two-piece ball is tough, and can also fly far. It has a solid core wrapped by a cover. Three-piece golf balls have rubber or liquid centers wrapped by elastic. Such balls create a large amount of spin, allowing a golfer to control the ball's flight when it is hit.

WHY DO GOLFERS "SLICE" THE BALL?

A slice is when the ball curves in the shape of a banana. Professional golfer Michelle Wie knows how to use the slice to get out of tough spots. She strikes the ball, causing it to spin sideways. Because Wie is right-handed, the ball starts heading left, and then swerves to the right. Wie and other golfers use the slice to hit around trees and ponds.

Two-piece ball

Three-piece ball

WHY DOES A SUPER BALL BOUNCE SO HIGH?

Super Balls are small, but they have a big bounce. That big bounce comes from compressing a hunk of synthetic, or human-made, rubber under a lot of pressure. Because the rubber is under so much pressure, it has a large amount of **potential energy**. That potential energy changes to kinetic energy when the ball bounces. As a result, a Super Ball bounces higher than an ordinary rubber ball.

Where did the **Hula-Hoop** idea come from?

Arthur "Spud" Melin and his friend, Richard Knerr, invented the Hula Hoop after they saw Australian children twirling wooden hoops around their waists. The pair gave their hip-swiveling plastic toy its famous name. The Hula-Hoop was a huge success for the toy company Wham-O. It sold 25 million hoops in the first four months of production in 1958.

What were the **first** Frisbees made of?

From 1871 until the 1950s, the Frisbie Baking Company of Bridgeport, Connecticut, sold pies to many New England colleges. Legend has it that a group of college students at Yale University in Connecticut took the empty tin pie plates—with the words "Frisbie's Pies" on them— and began tossing and catching them. In 1948, two men created a plastic version of a pie plate and called it a Pluto Platter. In 1957, Wham-O bought the rights to the Pluto Platter and soon changed the name to Frisbee in honor of the baking company that inspired the toy.

Which professional athletes have played more than two sports?

While many high school and college athletes have played more than one sport during the year, professional athletes usually play just one. There are exceptions, however. Bo Jackson was a running back for football's Los Angeles Raiders, and he also played baseball at different times for the Chicago White Sox, the California Angels, and the Kansas City Chiefs. Deion Sanders was another athlete who played pro football and baseball in the big leagues.

Bo Jackson played baseball and football.

In 2007, a Wagner T206 sold for $2.8 million.

WHICH ATHLETES HAVE PLAYED A PROFESSIONAL SPORT WITH ONE ARM?

The first one-armed pitcher to wear a baseball uniform was Pete Gray, who played for the St. Louis Browns. Gray's career was short-lived, however. When batting, he could not hit balls that curved because he had trouble stopping his swing with one arm. Jim Abbott, a stand-out pitcher, played with one arm for several teams, including the New York Yankees. Abbott was born without a right hand. After throwing the ball with his left hand, he quickly switched his glove—which was hanging on his right arm—to his left hand so he could catch the ball.

WHAT IS THE RAREST BASEBALL CARD?

A 1909 Honus Wagner T206 is the answer. Honus Wagner was a baseball player for the Pittsburgh Pirates. At that time, tobacco companies put baseball cards into their packages. Wagner didn't want his image used that way. When a tobacco company used his image without his permission, he stopped them from printing any more cards. Only a few had been made, making them very rare.

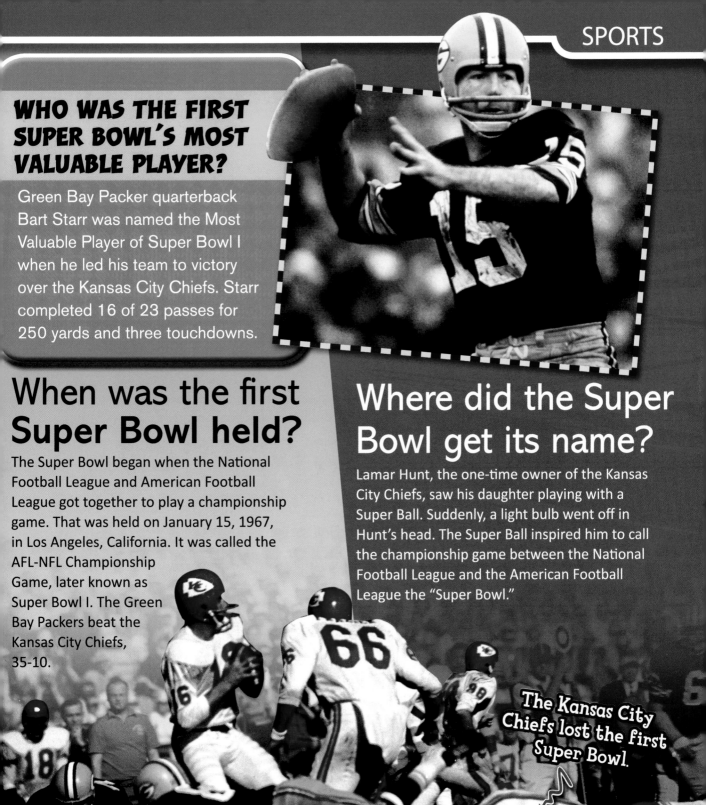

WHO WAS THE FIRST SUPER BOWL'S MOST VALUABLE PLAYER?

Green Bay Packer quarterback Bart Starr was named the Most Valuable Player of Super Bowl I when he led his team to victory over the Kansas City Chiefs. Starr completed 16 of 23 passes for 250 yards and three touchdowns.

When was the first Super Bowl held?

The Super Bowl began when the National Football League and American Football League got together to play a championship game. That was held on January 15, 1967, in Los Angeles, California. It was called the AFL-NFL Championship Game, later known as Super Bowl I. The Green Bay Packers beat the Kansas City Chiefs, 35-10.

Where did the Super Bowl get its name?

Lamar Hunt, the one-time owner of the Kansas City Chiefs, saw his daughter playing with a Super Ball. Suddenly, a light bulb went off in Hunt's head. The Super Ball inspired him to call the championship game between the National Football League and the American Football League the "Super Bowl."

The Kansas City Chiefs lost the first Super Bowl.

How can David Beckham make a soccer ball "bend"?

On October 6, 2001, English soccer player David Beckham made one of the great plays in soccer when he made a shot "bend." During the game against Greece, Beckham was given a free kick. He placed the ball about 89 feet (27 m) from the goal. Beckham then kicked the ball slightly off center with his left foot. The ball began to spin. As the spinning ball soared above the heads of the defensive line, it slowed and dipped into the goal. No one had ever seen anything like it. England won the game and qualified for the World Cup.

Soccer players don't want to get a red card.

WHAT DOES A RED CARD MEAN IN SOCCER?

Soccer referees give players red cards for making serious fouls. Once the referee gives a player a red card, the player is removed from the game and cannot be replaced, leaving that team one player short. Two yellow cards also equal a red.

WHY DO HOCKEY GOALIES WEAR MASKS?

Hockey goalies did not always wear face masks. In 1930, Clint Benedict, of the Montreal Maroons, first wore a mask in competition after a puck smashed into his face. He took the mask off after a few games. In 1959, Jacques Plante, the goaltender for the Montreal Canadiens, became the first goalie in NHL history to put on a face mask for good. Plante had been practicing with a fiberglass mask, but Canadien coach Toe Blake refused to allow Plante to wear it during the game. Three minutes into a game with the New York Rangers, a backhand shot split Plante's lip. He left for a few minutes, and returned wearing a mask.

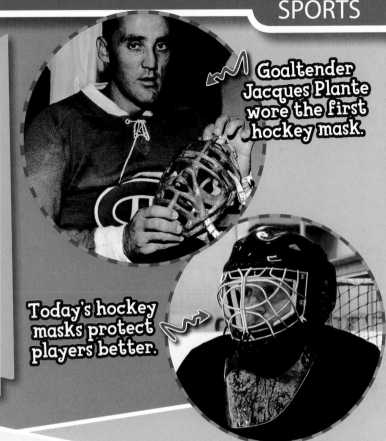

Goaltender Jacques Plante wore the first hockey mask.

Today's hockey masks protect players better.

How can hockey players quickly speed up on the ice?

Professional hockey players can reach speeds of more than 20 miles (32 km) per hour on the ice. Friction is one of the reasons they move so fast. When a player begins skating, he digs the blade of one of his skates into the ice and pushes forward. The friction between the gripping blade and the slippery ice creates resistance. That resistance allows a player to exert more energy into moving forward.

Why do racehorses wear blinders?

When running a race, a horse often wears a mask over its head. No, they are not getting ready for Halloween. The masks, called blinders, block a horse's peripheral vision— the ability to see things out of the corner of the eye. This lets the animal focus all of its attention on the track in front of it.

WHY DO HORSES WEAR SHOES?

Just as your shoes protect the bottoms of your feet, horseshoes are designed to protect a horse's feet. Humans nail or glue the shoes onto the animal's hooves.

Horses wear shoes nailed to their hooves.

Why do racehorses run counterclockwise?

The reason dates back to the American Revolution. In 1780, William Whitley of Kentucky opened the first circular horse racetrack in America. A patriot, Whitley had the horses run counterclockwise to rebel against the British whose racehorses ran clockwise. Whitley's tradition remained when runners and cars took to the track.

Why does Michael **Phelps** wear a special swim suit?

World-class swimmers such as Michael Phelps make swimming look easy. Phelps overcomes the effects of drag created by the water by being in great physical shape and by wearing a high-tech suit that allows water to flow over his body with less resistance.

Michael Phe... in a high-te... swim sui...

WHY IS MICHAEL PHELPS AN OLYMPIC SUPERSTAR?

Michael Phelps has won 14 career Olympic gold medals, the most by any Olympian. He also holds the record for winning the most gold medals in a single Olympics. He won eight at the 2008 Games in Beijing, China.

speedo

Janet Guthrie was a top female race car driver.

Who was the first woman to race in the Indianapolis 500?

Long before Danica Patrick became a famous race car driver, Janet Guthrie was the first woman to compete in the Indianapolis 500. The Indy 500 is one of racing's most important events. Guthrie raced in 1977. The year before, she also became the first woman to compete in NASCAR's Daytona 500.

WHO WAS THE FIRST FEMALE TO UMPIRE A MAJOR LEAGUE BASEBALL GAME?

"You're Outtttttttttttttttt!" In 1989, Pam Postema made history when she uttered those words. Postema was the first female to umpire a major league baseball game. The game was an exhibition and did not count. In 2007, Ria Cortesio became the second female umpire to work during a major league exhibition game. The game was between the Chicago Cubs and the Arizona Diamondbacks. No woman umpire has ever worked a regular-season game in the major leagues.

WHO WAS THE FIRST WOMAN TO ANNOUNCE AN NFL GAME?

In 1987, Gayle Sierens, a TV news anchor in Tampa, Florida, was the first woman to announce an NFL game. She was also the last. Sierens had once been a sportscaster. In the mid-1980s, an executive at NBC Sports thought a woman should call an NFL game. Sierens went to Missouri to broadcast a Seattle Seahawks-Kansas City Chiefs game. The reviews were good. NBC offered Sierens the opportunity to call six more games, but her bosses at the local TV station said she'd have to give up her anchor job if she accepted, so she turned down NBC's offer.

Which thoroughbred racehorse is the fastest of all time?

Secretariat has the honor of being the fastest racehorse of all time. In 1973, Secretariat ran in the Belmont Stakes by completing the 1½-mile (2.41 km) course in 2 minutes 24 seconds. When Secretariat crossed the finish line, he was an amazing 31 lengths ahead of his closest challengers. The horse had already won the Kentucky Derby with a time of 1 minute 59 seconds. Secretariat also won the Preakness, another famous race. The champion earned the Triple Crown, U.S. horse racing's greatest honor, for winning all three of those races in the same year.

Who is the fastest human?

In September 2009, Usain Bolt, from Jamaica, became the fastest human in the world. He ran the 100-meter dash in 9.58 seconds, shattering the old record of 9.69 seconds.

WHY WAS SECRETARIAT SO FAST?

Experts say that Secretariat was so fast because he had a 22-pound (9.97 kg) heart, more than twice the size of a typical thoroughbred's heart.

185

Did You Know?

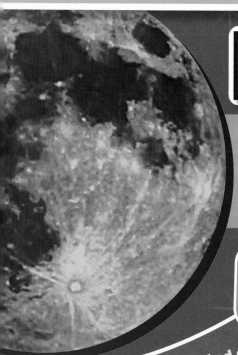

The moon's color as seen from Earth depends on the amount of dust in Earth's atmosphere. Sometimes the moon looks yellow or orange.

Hawaii is moving toward Japan at about 3.94 inches (10 cm) a year.

The closest stars to Earth are Alpha and Proxima Centauri, which are 4.3 light years away. A light year is the distance light travels in one year—5.88 trillion miles (9.46 trillion km).

Scientists have invented a dress that senses whether the wearer is happy or sad. The Bubelle dress uses sensors to detect your mood. The dress then changes color to match what you are feeling.

The average human heart beats around 100,000 times a day.

Infants blink only once a minute.

Japan is the country with the highest life expectancy. Japanese live on average, 82 years.

Capuchin monkeys can live to be 40 years old.

According to legend, Rome was founded by Romulus and Remus, brothers who were raised by a wolf.

Some blind people use miniature horses as guide animals.

Researchers at the Massachusetts Institute of Technology have invented electric cars that stack together like shopping carts.

More people speak Chinese than any other language.

A volcanic rock known as pumice is the only rock that can float in water.

The most common backyard bird in the U.S. is the northern cardinal.

People in Thailand, Laos, Nepal, and Sri Lanka ride elephants rather than horses when they play polo.

Web sites:

Animals

The Animal Planet's http://animal.discovery.com/ is neat. There are games, videos, and blogs.

Earth

Take a wonderful journey across the globe with this Web site from the Smithsonian Institution. http://www.mnh.si.edu/earth/main_frames.html.

Space

NASA's Web sites are out of this world. Check out http://solarsystem.nasa.gov/planets/index.cfm and learn more about our solar system. Click on a planet and discover amazing facts.

Humans

Go to http://kidshealth.org/kid/htbw/htbw_main_page.html and learn how the human body works.

People and Places

Explore the world on http://www.nationalgeographic.com/. This amazing Web site links to parts of the world many people don't know about. You can access news features, maps, videos, and learn about many different people and places. For the latest news about people and places, go to timeforkids.com.

History

If you're a history buff, go to http://www.history.com/. Click on "This Day in History" to find out what happened on any particular day. Learn about world leaders and play dozens of games.

Science

Read more about the world of science with National Geographic at http://science.nationalgeographic.com/science/.

Technology

If you're interested in some of the dumbest inventions ever produced, the editors of *Life* magazine have put them all together for you at http://www.life.com/image/3270485/in-gallery/25371.

Arts and Culture

If you're interested in the art of the Renaissance, http://www.renaissanceconnection.org/home.html is a wonderful place to learn about how Renaissance artists lived and worked.

Sports

Sports and kids go together like, well, sports and kids. Keep up with all the news of sports and play some games at http://www.sikids.com/.

Book List:

Animals

National Geographic Encyclopedia of Animals by Karen McGhee & George McKay, PhD. (National Geographic Society, 2006)

Earth

Smithsonian Earth by James F. Luhr (Dorling Kindersley Publishing, 2007)

Space

Smithsonian Atlas of Space Exploration by Roger D. Launius & Andrew K. Johnston (Smithsonian Institution, 2009)

Humans

Human Body: An Interactive Guide to the Inner Workings of the Body (Barron's Educational Series, 2008)

People and Places

History of the World: People, Places, and Ideas by Henry Billing (Steck-Vaughn Company, 2003)

History

Children's Encyclopedia of American History by David C. King (Smithsonian Institution, 2003)

Science

The Science Book: Everything You Need to Know About the World and How It Works by Marshall Brain (National Geographic, 2008)

Technology

Computers and Technology by Tara Koellhoffer, (Editor) & Emily Sohn (Forward) (Chelsea Clubhouse, 2006)

Arts and Culture

Performing Arts (Culture Encyclopedia) by Antony Mason (Mason Crest Publishers, 2002)

Sports

The Greatest Moments in Sports by Len Berman (Sourcebooks, 2009)

abdomen the part of the body that contains the organs needed for digestion

air pressure the weight of the atmosphere that pushes down on people and objects

aerodynamics the forces exerted by air or other gases in motion

antenna a metallic device used for sending and receiving radio waves

antibodies proteins in the body that fight off disease and infection

bacteria microscopic single-celled organisms found in water, air, and soil

bioluminescent relating to animals that make their own light

botanist a scientist who studies plants

buoyancy the ability of an object to float or rise when submerged in a fluid

camouflage a method that allows an organism to blend into its environment, avoiding detection

cartilage a flexible, rubbery tissue that cushions bones and joints

caste any of four main social classes into which Hindu society is divided

centrifugal force the force directed away from the center of a revolving body

cerebellum a part of the brain that controls muscle movement and balance

chlorophyll the green pigment in plants responsible for the absorption of light energy during photosynthesis

circulatory system the organs and tissues that help pump blood and oxygen through the body

city-state a self-governing state, such as those in ancient Greece, consisting of a city and surrounding land

compounds the combination of two or more elements

conduction the movement of heat energy from one object to another

decompose the process by which a dead organism rots away

deforestation the cutting down of huge stretches of forest

dehydration the process by which a body loses more fluids than it takes in

digestive tract the system of organs, including the stomach and intestines, responsible for breaking food down so that the body can absorb nutrients

DNA short for deoxyribonucleic acid; DNA is a spiral-shaped molecule found in the body's cells. It contains a person's genes, which determine characteristics, such as eye and hair color.

domesticated adapted to live with humans

drag the resistance to a moving body created by rushing air or water

ecological relating to an organism's relationship with the environment

elliptical egg-shaped

embryo early developmental stage of an animal or plant following the fertilization of an egg cell; In humans, the term embryo describes the fertilized egg during its first seven weeks of existence.

enzyme a substance produced by cells that speeds up the chemical reactions necessary for life

epicenter the point on Earth's surface that lies directly above the focus of an earthquake

erosion the gradual wearing down of soil

evolution the theory that various plants and animals change over time to a different and usually more complex or better form

executive the branch of government responsible for the enforcement of the laws passed by the legislative branch of government; In the United States, the President is head of the executive branch.

fetus a term that describes the human embryo after eight weeks of development

fossil fuels fuels, such as oil and coal that are created by plant and animal matter over millions of years

friction the force that one surface exerts on another when the two rub against each other

glaciers large masses of compacted snow and ice

glucose sugar in plants that is used as food for energy

gravity the force of attraction between two objects

greenhouse gas a gas such as carbon dioxide, methane, and nitrous oxide, that contributes to global warming

hemangioma a mass of blood vessels that appear as birthmarks

hyperactivity unusually active

hypothesis an educated guess

immune system cells, proteins, and tissue that protect the body from infection and disease

integrated open to everyone regardless of race

judicial the branch of government, including courts and judges, responsible for interpreting laws passed by the legislative branch of government

kinetic energy the energy of movement

legislative the branch of government that makes laws

lens a part of the eye that helps bring rays of light into focus

levees an embankment that helps protect against flooding

magnetic fields the lines of force surrounding the sun and the planets generated by electrical currents

magnitude total amount of energy released during an earthquake

mammal a warm-blooded vertebrate (having a backbone) that has hair or fur; Mammals feed milk to their young.

mantle largest layer of Earth's interior between the crust and the core

matter anything that has mass and can be measured; There are three types of matter: solids, liquids, and gases.

melanin a pigment that produces eye, skin, and hair color

metamorphosis a period during the life cycle of many insects, most amphibians, and some fish, during which the individual body changes from one form to another

migration movement

mucus a fluid formed in the body that lubricates and protects

mutations changes in genes produced by a change in the DNA that makes up the hereditary material of all living organisms

mythological stories that lack a factual basis

mythology a group of myths or legends belonging to a particular culture

network two or more computers that are linked by wires or cables

nuclei (plural of nucleus) the positively charged central part of an atom

ozone layer a layer of the upper atmosphere that absorbs harmful ultraviolet radiation from the sun and keeps it from reaching Earth's surface

palate the roof of a person's or animal's mouth

particulates small airborne particles

pheromones chemicals produced by an animal that affect the behavior of other animals

photons small points of light

photosynthesis the process by which green plants trap light and energy to form carbohydrates

pigment any colors in plant or animal cells

pistons metal cylinders that slide up and down in an engine

pitch a property of sound that represents the frequency of the sound

plate tectonics the theory that explains the moving, or drifting, of Earth's continents

pollen a powdery substance produced by flowers

pollination the transfer of individual pollen grains from the male part of a plant to the female part of the plant that makes fertilization possible

pollution contamination of air, water, or soil by substances that are harmful to living organisms

potential energy stored energy

prey an animal that is hunted by another animal

primates animals that include humans, apes, monkeys, and lemurs

prisms cut glass objects that can separate white light into many colors

rectum the lower part of the large intestine

refraction bending of a light wave

resolution the quality of detail in an image

respiratory system the organs in the body responsible for breathing—the taking in of oxygen and the exhaling of carbon dioxide

retina light sensitive tissue located at the back of the eyeball

rituals habits or customs

secede to break away from, or leave

siege to surround a place in order to force a surrender

sit-in a type of demonstration during the Civil Rights movement in which protesters refused to leave a particular building or area

sphenisciformes a group of birds, including penguins, that cannot fly

spires tall, narrow pointed structures located on the tops of buildings or towers

storm surge a rise of water created by high winds

symbiotic the relationship between two different species of organisms that benefit one another

synchronous rotation a term that describes how the moon (or any other orbiting body), takes as long to rotate on its axis as it does to make one orbit around another orbiting body (such as the Earth)

ultraviolet radiation electromagnetic radiation invisible to the human eye

urushiol a toxic oil found in plants such as poison ivy

vertebrates animals with backbones

viruses tiny particles, smaller than bacteria, that can cause a variety of illnesses by entering a person's body through the nose, mouth, or breaks in the skin

wavelength the distance from the crest, or high point of one sound, or electromagnetic wave, to the next

Aborigines 89
Adams, John 86
airplane 138, 143
American Revolution 84, 109, 120, 182
Antarctica 13, 31, 38
antibiotics 61
apes 7
aspirin 61
atmosphere 24, 25, 30, 32, 34, 36, 40, 43, 44, 45, 51, 54
Australia 36, 89, 177

bacteria 19, 61, 63, 68, 69, 70, 72, 75, 122, 129, 142
baseball 100, 162, 170, 172, 173, 178, 184
basketball 165, 174
bats 8
Beckham, David 180
bees 126
Bell, Alexander Graham 147
Berlin Wall 115
birds 13, 22
blood 8, 18, 19, 44, 62, 63, 64, 65, 68, 69, 71, 73, 78, 146
Bolt, Usain 185
Brazil 88

camera 146
cats 12, 20, 158
cell phone 138
Charlie Brown 154
chemical reaction 125
Chicago 92
China, Great Wall of 82
Chunnel 83
Civil War, U.S. 97, 112, 161
clouds 30, 34, 132
Cold War 115
Columbus, Christopher 106
comet 41, 47
Communism 115
crayons 151
Crusades 103

curling 164

Dali, Salvador 156
Darwin, Charles 110
deserts 87
diamonds 39
Didrikson, Babe 163
dogs 6, 12, 19, 20, 74
Dr. Seuss 158

ear wax 69
Easter Island 88
echolocation 8
Edison, Thomas 153
Egypt 93
Eiffel Tower 95
Einstein, Albert 55
e-mail 137
Erikson, Leif 102
evolution 9, 110

fingerprints 76
football 162, 166, 171, 178, 179
Forbidden City 81
freckles 71
friction 33, 35, 54, 128, 142, 167, 169, 173, 181
Frisbee 177

Gandhi, Mohandas 97
gasoline 149
Geisel, Theodore 158
Gettysburg Address 120
Golden Gate Bridge 83
golf 176
Grand Canyon 26
gravity 31, 40, 42, 46, 47, 49, 50, 51, 52, 135
Great Depression 116
Green Bay Packers 171, 179
Gutenberg, Johannes 104
Guthrie, Janet 184

Hale, Nathan 120
hay fever 60
HDTV 139

helicopter 143
hockey 181
Homer Simpson 59
Hula-Hoop 177
Hundred Years War 105
hurricane 37
hyperactivity 130
hypothesis 6

igneous rock 39
Industrial Revolution 107
insects 11, 15, 18, 19, 23

Jackson, Bo 178
Jefferson, Thomas 86
Jupiter 47, 54, 134

Kansas City Chiefs 178, 179
King, Martin Luther Jr. 97

Lincoln, Abraham 112, 120
London Bridge 80

Madison, Dolly 86
Marconi, Guglielmo 140
Mars 44, 47, 48, 54
Mariana Trench 90
Maya 100
metamorphic rock 39
meteors 24, 43, 54
Mickey Mouse 154
microwave 142
Milky Way 52
Mona Lisa 157
moon 18, 31, 33, 43, 45, 46, 47, 48, 49, 53, 55, 154
Morse, Samuel 147
Moses, Grandma 156
Mount Everest 38
MTV 153
mummies 93
mutations 20

Naismith, James Dr. 165
NASCAR 167, 168, 184

Navajo 118
Neptune 47, 49, 51
New York 31, 36, 92, 120, 140, 152, 156, 170, 172, 178, 181
Niagara Falls 91

Olympics 163, 175, 183

Parthenon 95
pencils 150, 151
penguins 13, 31
Phelps, Michael, 183
pheromones 14
Picasso, Pablo 157
Pluto 49, 51
pollution 94
Pompeii 99
Portuguese 88, 121
Potter, Harry 159
primates 7
printing press 104

quicksand 35

radio 138, 140
Revere, Paul 109
Rickey, Branch 170
Ride, Sally 45
Robinson, Jackie 170
Rome 98
Roosevelt, Franklin 116, 119
Rowling, J.K. 159

Saturn 47, 51
Schiaparelli, Giovanni 44
Secretariat 185
sedimentary rock 39
Shakespeare, William 160
slavery 86, 97, 111, 112, 161
sneeze 61, 72
Snoopy 154
soap 133
soccer 180
solar system 41, 42, 46, 47, 49, 51, 52
Sputnik 45

Starr, Bart 179
Statue of Liberty 84
sun 24, 26, 30, 31, 34, 36, 40, 41, 42, 43, 46, 47, 49, 50, 51, 53, 54, 71
Super Ball 177, 179
Super Bowl 179
sweat 67, 68

tectonic plates 28, 38
telegraph 147
Tereshkova, Valentina 45
Three Gorges Dam 83
Times Square 152
Titanic 113
tornado 25
Trojan War 101
Truman, Harry 117
tsunamis 33
Tubman, Harriet 111

U.S. Capitol 85, 86
Underground Railroad 111

vaccines 148
Venice, Italy 80
vertebrates 9
Vikings 102
volcano 27, 99

Wagner, Honus 178
Warhol, Andy 156
Washington, George 85, 86, 108, 120
Wheaties 163
White House 85, 86
Wie, Michelle 176
World Series 172
World War I 114
World War II 115, 116, 117, 118, 119
Wright, Orville 143
Wright, Wilbur 143

x-ray 148

Zamboni 162